MACMILLAN MASTER GUIDES

MASTER GUIDES

GENERAL EDITOR: JAMES GIBSON

JANE AUSTEN	*Emma* Norman Page *Sense and Sensibility* Judy Simons *Persuasion* Judy Simons *Pride and Prejudice* Raymond Wilson *Mansfield Park* Richard Wirdnam
SAMUEL BECKETT	*Waiting for Godot* Jennifer Birkett
WILLIAM BLAKE	*Songs of Innocence and Songs of Experience* Alan Tomlinson
ROBERT BOLT	*A Man for All Seasons* Leonard Smith
CHARLOTTE BRONTË	*Jane Eyre* Robert Miles
EMILY BRONTË	*Wuthering Heights* Hilda D. Spear
JOHN BUNYAN	*The Pilgrim's Progress* Beatrice Batson
GEOFFREY CHAUCER	*The Miller's Tale* Michael Alexander *The Pardoner's Tale* Geoffrey Lester *The Wife of Bath's Tale* Nicholas Marsh *The Knight's Tale* Anne Samson *The Prologue to the Canterbury Tales* Nigel Thomas and Richard Swan
JOSEPH CONRAD	*The Secret Agent* Andrew Mayne
CHARLES DICKENS	*Bleak House* Dennis Butts *Great Expectations* Dennis Butts *Hard Times* Norman Page
GEORGE ELIOT	*Middlemarch* Graham Handley *Silas Marner* Graham Handley *The Mill on the Floss* Helen Wheeler
T. S. ELIOT	*Murder in the Cathedral* Paul Lapworth *Selected Poems* Andrew Swarbrick
HENRY FIELDING	*Joseph Andrews* Trevor Johnson
E. M. FORSTER	*A Passage to India* Hilda D. Spear *Howards End* Ian Milligan
WILLIAM GOLDING	*The Spire* Rosemary Sumner *Lord of the Flies* Raymond Wilson
OLIVER GOLDSMITH	*She Stoops to Conquer* Paul Ranger
THOMAS HARDY	*The Mayor of Casterbridge* Ray Evans *Tess of the d'Urbervilles* James Gibson *Far from the Madding Crowd* Colin Temblett-Wood
BEN JONSON	*Volpone* Michael Stout
JOHN KEATS	*Selected Poems* John Garrett
RUDYARD KIPLING	*Kim* Leonée Ormond
PHILIP LARKIN	*The Less Deceived* and *The Whitsun Weddings* Andrew Swarbrick

MACMILLAN MASTER GUIDES

D.H. LAWRENCE	*Sons and Lovers* R. P. Draper
HARPER LEE	*To Kill a Mockingbird* Jean Armstrong
LAURIE LEE	*Cider with Rosie* Brian Tarbitt
GERARD MANLEY HOPKINS	*Selected Poems* R. J. C. Watt
CHRISTOPHER MARLOWE	*Doctor Faustus* David A. Male
THE METAPHYSICAL POETS	Joan van Emden
THOMAS MIDDLETON and WILLIAM ROWLEY	*The Changeling* Tony Bromham
ARTHUR MILLER	*The Crucible* Leonard Smith *Death of a Salesman* Peter Spalding
GEORGE ORWELL	*Animal Farm* Jean Armstrong
WILLIAM SHAKESPEARE	*Richard II* Charles Barber *Othello* Tony Bromham *Hamlet* Jean Brooks *King Lear* Francis Casey *Henry V* Peter Davison *The Winter's Tale* Diana Devlin *Julius Caesar* David Elloway *Macbeth* David Elloway *The Merchant of Venice* A. M. Kinghorn *Measure for Measure* Mark Lilly *Henry IV Part I* Helen Morris *Romeo and Juliet* Helen Morris *A Midsummer Night's Dream* Kenneth Pickering *The Tempest* Kenneth Pickering *Coriolanus* Gordon Williams *Antony and Cleopatra* Martin Wine *Twelfth Night* R. P. Draper
GEORGE BERNARD SHAW	*St Joan* Leonée Ormond
RICHARD SHERIDAN	*The School for Scandal* Paul Ranger *The Rivals* Jeremy Rowe
ALFRED TENNYSON	*In Memoriam* Richard Gill
EDWARD THOMAS	*Selected Poems* Gerald Roberts
ANTHONY TROLLOPE	*Barchester Towers* K. M. Newton
JOHN WEBSTER	*The White Devil* and *The Duchess of Malfi* David A. Male
VIRGINIA WOOLF	*To the Lighthouse* John Mepham *Mrs Dalloway* Julian Pattison
WILLIAM WORDSWORTH	*The Prelude Books I and II* Helen Wheeler

MACMILLAN MASTER GUIDES
THE SECRET AGENT
BY JOSEPH CONRAD

ANDREW MAYNE

© Andrew Mayne 1987

All rights reserved. No reproduction, copy or transmission of
this publication may be made without written permission.

No paragraph of this publication may be reproduced, copied or
transmitted save with written permission or in accordance with
the provisions of the Copyright, Designs and Patents Act 1988,
or under the terms of any licence permitting limited copying
issued by the Copyright Licensing Agency, 90 Tottenham Court
Road, London W1P 9HE.

Any person who does any unauthorised act in relation to this
publication may be liable to criminal prosecution and civil
claims for damages.

First published 1987 by
THE MACMILLAN PRESS LTD
Houndmills, Basingstoke, Hampshire RG21 2XS
and London
Companies and representatives
throughout the world

ISBN 0–333–43275–4

A catalogue record for this book is available
from the British Library.

Reprinted 1994

Printed in China

CONTENTS

General editor's preface and acknowledgements   vi

1	**Joseph Conrad: biographical outline**			1
2	**Sources and background**	2.1	The Greenwich Bomb Outrage 1894	6
		2.2	Anarchism and the political background	7
3	**Summaries and critical commentaries**	3.1	General summary of the plot	10
		3.2	Chapter summaries and commentaries	12
4	**Themes and issues**	4.1	Facing the darkness	51
		4.2	Mistaken perspectives	54
		4.3	Self-interest	56
		4.4	Social and political views	58
		4.5	Science	60
		4.6	Time	62
5	**Characterisation**	5.1	The Verloc household	66
		5.2	The revolutionaries	68
		5.3	The public domain	70
6	**Technical features**	6.1	Narrative structure	74
		6.2	Irony	76
		6.3	Conrad's narrator	78
7	**Specimen passage and commentary**			80
8	**Critical reception**			84

Revision questions   87

Further reading   89

GENERAL EDITOR'S PREFACE

The aim of the Macmillan Master Guides is to help you to appreciate the book you are studying by providing information about it and by suggesting ways of reading and thinking about it which will lead to a fuller understanding. The section on the writer's life and background has been designed to illustrate those aspects of the writer's life which have influenced the work, and to place it in its personal and literary context. The summaries and critical commentary are of special importance in that each brief summary of the action is followed by an examination of the significant critical points. The space which might have been given to repetitive explanatory notes has been devoted to a detailed analysis of the kind of passage which might confront you in an examination. Literary criticism is concerned with both the broader aspects of the work being studied and with its detail. The ideas which meet us in reading a great work of literature, and their relevance to us today, are an essential part of our study, and our Guides look at the thought of their subject in some detail. But just as essential is the craft with which the writer has constructed his work of art, and this may be considered under several technical headings — characterisation, language, style and stagecraft, for example.

The authors of these Guides are all teachers and writers of wide experience, and they have chosen to write about books they admire and know well in the belief that they can communicate their admiration to you. But you yourself must read and know intimately the book you are studying. No one can do that for you. You should see this book as a lamp-post. Use it to shed light, not to lean against. If you know your text and know what it is saying about life, and how it says it, then you will enjoy it, and there is no better way of passing an examination in literature.

JAMES GIBSON

Acknowledgements

All the quotations from *The Secret Agent* are taken from the text of the novel published by Penguin.

Cover illustration: *Cabyard at Night* by Robert Polhill Bevan. Photograph © Brighton City Art Galleries.

1 JOSEPH CONRAD: BIOGRAPHICAL OUTLINE

Joseph Conrad (1857–1924), christened Józef Teodor Konrad Korzeniowski, was born in the Ukraine, which at the time was a part of Poland under Russian domination. His background was the landowning nobility, and both his parents were fervent Polish nationalists. Their home in Warsaw became a meeting place for those working for the cause of Polish nationalism, and when Conrad was four, his father, Apollo, who had been involved in underground activities against the Russians, was arrested and exiled to the near arctic conditions of Vologda in Northern Russia. Conrad was later to assert, 'My father was no revolutionary . . . in the sense of working for the subversion of any social or political scheme. He was simply a patriot.' Conrad's mother, who insisted on accompanying her husband into exile with the young Conrad, was to die three years later, largely as a result of the climate. Apollo, a writer and translator of some reputation, took charge of his son's education, but away from his homeland Apollo was always struggling against depression and deprivation. When his father died in 1869, Conrad, at the age of eleven, passed to the care of an uncle, Thaddeus Bobrowski, a man who took his duties seriously as Conrad's guardian. However, the sternly level-headed Bobrowski could not dissuade Conrad from his resolution to leave Poland to go to sea. Such seems to have been his dream for some time. Clearly, he had a thirst for adventure, though there were some sounder reasons behind his desire to leave Poland. There was little to look forward to as the orphaned son of a patriot exiled for agitation against a foreign power which still ruled Poland; moreover, Conrad risked conscription into the Russian army. He felt a natural desire to show his independence, and so, overriding the opposition of his relations who frowned on this demeaning of himself to the life of a seaman, in 1874 Conrad left for Marseilles. He seems to have chosen a French port because French was a second language for him – as it was for most cultivated Poles – and his uncle appears to have had some influence in the shipping industry in this Mediterranean port.

So began an exciting period in Conrad's life, though there were also times of idleness and indulgence. Conrad appears to have been a rather extravagant and highly-strung young man who was always short of money – a problem that was to persist for much of his life. Letters from his uncle constantly took him to task for his wild spending of limited financial resources. Indeed, after sailing to the West Indies first as a passenger and later as an apprentice seaman, Conrad squandered all his money on some reckless smuggling scheme and then on gambling; he attempted suicide, and his long-suffering uncle had to come to his rescue, paying out some 3,000 francs to clear the young man's debts. Nevertheless, Bobrowski's opinion of Conrad was not totally unfavourable: 'My study of the Individual has convinced me that he is not a bad boy, only one who is extremely sensitive, conceited, reserved, and in addition excitable.' His uncle certainly brought home to Conrad his responsibilities – 'You were idling for nearly a whole year – you fell into debt, you deliberately shot yourself' – and it seemed time for a new departure.

In 1878 Conrad joined his first British ship; its home port was in Suffolk. The significance of this change of flag can hardly be overemphasised, not least because, if Conrad had not joined the English Merchant Marine, our literature would probably have been denied one of its finest novelists. At this time Conrad reported that he did not know more than six words of English. The next phase of Conrad's life sees him serving in a number of ships and moving steadily through the various stages of seamanship, ranging from able seaman to captain. By 1886 he had passed his examination for master mariner, and in that same year he was naturalised as a British subject. In a period of twelve years, until he gave up the sea and sought a literary career, Conrad served on ships sailing to Singapore and the various jungle ports of Borneo; he worked on the fast passenger clippers sailing to Australia and saw much of the Malay archipelago where many of his sea stories were to be set. He never stayed long with any single ship; often his reasons for giving up jobs were rather obscure. His only actual command was the *Ottago* which he took over in Bangkok after the former captain's death – an experience which was to provide him with material for one of his best tales, *The Secret Sharer*.

There was one important interlude in his career in the British Merchant Marine. This occurred in 1890 when Conrad made arrangements, largely it seems on a romantic impulse, to go to the Congo and pilot a river boat – 'a sardine can with a stern wheel' – for a Belgian colonial company. It was an experience which revealed to Conrad the extremes of colonial exploitation (he was to use it as the basis for his *Heart of Darkness*) and it did much to undermine his health and cut short his sea career, though during his last years at sea Conrad had already begun to hanker after a literary career and he had started work on a novel which was to become his first work, *Almayer's Folly*. The novel was published in 1896, a year after Conrad had left his last position as a seaman and settled in England.

In 1896 Conrad married Jessie George; the couple were to have two sons, though at the time of their marriage Conrad imagined that he had not very long to live. The Conrads moved frequently from home to home, money was often short and Conrad's health went repeatedly through bad periods. His wide experience of life at sea had given him a peculiar richness of material as a writer; he provides an extreme example of the fact that many of our greatest English novelists have come from outside the social mainstream. Yet his detachment from certain aspects of English life could be a weakness at first as well as a strength later on in his career. Writing cost him enormous nervous strain. Reading many of his letters one is often horrified by the cost he paid in personal terms for his creative work, even allowing for a certain self-dramatising tendency in him.

Conrad's early writing was based largely on his experiences at sea. By common critical assent, his first major achievement was *The Nigger of the Narcissus* (1897) which, along with *Youth* (1902), *Heart of Darkness* (1902) and *Typhoon* (1903), showed his mastery of the *novella* or 'long short story'. In these early tales, the narrative is centred on a particular voyage which gives the stories clearly defined structural limits, while a study of the life of men on board a ship provides Conrad with a microcosm of human existence and a laboratory in which he can atomise the human spirit as it faces testing experiences. Again and again Conrad writes of men *in extremis*, in the belief that in order to discover what is most significant about human nature a man must first be isolated from the usual supports of civilisation and be forced back on his own resources.

Conrad was always preoccupied with the formal requirements of a narrative; how the story was to be told and what narrative point of view was to be adopted were always paramount questions. Marlow, a retired seaman of wide experience and sympathy, first appeared in *Youth*, and Conrad was to make good use of his services as a first-person narrator, perhaps most notably in *Heart of Darkness*. It is Marlow who narrates most of *Lord Jim* (1900); this work was Conrad's first long novel, though it had started life as a short story, and its somewhat laboured drawing out of its material from an originally smaller conception is apparent in the final product. The central incident of the novel concerns Jim's sudden and barely consciously conceived decision when, as chief mate on the *Patna*, he abandons what seems to be a sinking ship and leaves a party of pilgrim passengers to their fate. Marlow and other narrator-characters endlessly debate and attempt to analyse the motivation of this act and its repercussions on the life of Jim, a man who had idealistically conceived a heroic destiny for himself.

With the publication of *Nostromo* in 1904, Conrad's writing took a new direction. It was his first book which was not located in a setting of which he had detailed personal knowledge. Adopting a lofty, omniscient manner of narration and making use of shifts in time and perspective, Conrad creates with masterly imaginative detail the Occidental Province of the Latin American state of Costaguana. The novel has at its centre the theme of the corrupting influence of material interests. Costaguana is inveterately unstable, and the successful working of the San Tomé silver mine, far from bringing a measure of law and order, inevitably attracts the parasitic attentions of the country's administrators and politicians. Disillusionment and the impermanence of human ideals in the face of an indifferent universe are the keynotes of a novel in which nearly all the major characters are subjected to various kinds of testing experiences – and are found wanting.

At the time of writing *The Secret Agent*, which was published in 1907, Conrad was still drained from the effort that had gone into his masterpiece, *Nostromo*. The health of his wife Jessie, who was pregnant, was poor – after a fall in 1904 she was to be a semi-cripple for the rest of her life – and though Conrad's work had enjoyed a *succès d'estime*, popular success and financial security eluded him. (For some further information about the contemporary reception of Conrad's novels, turn to p.84). Yet this was one of the richest periods of Conrad's creative life. His next major achievement, *Under Western Eyes* (1911), is particularly relevant to a study of *The Secret Agent* for, set in Russia and Switzerland, it deals with the betrayals and violence of European revolutionary life and extends and develops many of the political preoccupations of the earlier novels of this middle period. Once again, at the centre of the novel is the theme of the corruptibility of man. Razumov, a Russian student, is drawn into betraying a revolutionary acquaintance who seeks his aid at a time of crisis, and as a consequence Razumov finds himself enmeshed in a life of deception: exiled revolutionists who do not know of Razumov's act of betrayal regard him as a hero, whereas in reality he has been compelled to act as an agent of the Tsarist regime.

The publication of *Chance* in 1913 at last saw Conrad gaining his first popular and financial success, and by the time of his death in 1924 the former Polish seaman was well established as a leading figure in the English literary world. *Victory* (1915) and *The Shadow-Line* (1917) are remarkable achievements, but Conrad's later work, such as *The Rover* (1923) shows something of a decline. In fact, by the time his books began to sell in any numbers, Conrad had already made his outstanding contribution to English literature, in tales such as *Heart of Darkness* and *The Secret Sharer* and in those three great novels of his middle period, *Nostromo*, *The Secret Agent* and *Under Western Eyes*.

2 SOURCES AND BACKGROUND

2.1 THE GREENWICH BOMB OUTRAGE, 1894

In his 'Author's Note' Conrad locates one of the sources of *The Secret Agent* in 'a few words uttered by a friend in casual conversation' about anarchism in general and the particular incident of the bomb attempt on the Greenwich Observatory (1894). The friend was probably Ford Madox Ford, a fellow novelist, who had some acquaintance with anarchists and who later claimed to have provided Conrad with much material for the novel's plot. In fact, Conrad was invariably more than a shade devious when it came to describing his sources, and his account in the Note is to be viewed with as much suspicion as Ford's own claims. It is likely that Conrad had read contemporary reports of the Greenwich Outrage of 1894 and knew much more about the affair than his casual reference to it suggests. In *Conrad's Western World* (1971), Norman Sherry provides an extended investigation of the background and historical sources of *The Secret Agent*; it seems, for instance, that Conrad was familiar with some anarchist publications, of the kind that are on sale in Verloc's shop, besides the book of recollections by the retired assistant commissioner of police which is mentioned in the 'Author's Note'. This work, *Sidelights on the Home Rule Movement* by Sir Robert Anderson, as well as providing the statement about secrecy which Conrad suggests stuck in his mind, also added to his knowledge of the use of police agents against Fenian activity.

The Greenwich Bomb Outrage remains somewhat mysterious. Of course, the sense that 'it was impossible to fathom its origin by any reasonable or even unreasonable process of thought' was what, Conrad records, first struck his imagination. The central facts of the affair are that one Martial Bourdin was found in Greenwich Park on 15 February 1894, as *The Times* reported, 'in a kneeling posture, terribly mutilated'; one hand had been blown off in an explosion which had been set off prematurely and by accident. Bourdin, a very short, fair man of about thirty, 'died in less than an hour'. It seems that Bourdin's brother-in-law, Samuels, who was editor of a notorious anarchist newspaper and an advocate of 'direct action', and yet probably a police agent, had acted as an *agent provocateur* by instigating the abortive operation. Thus it is likely that no anarchists were responsible for the explosion; it appears that they were just as worried about its consequences as their counterparts in the novel.

Readers who are interested in discovering more about the background to the novel should consult Norman Sherry's study and the essay by Ian Watt at the end of the Macmillan Casebook on *The Secret Agent*. Conrad certainly liked to set a story going in his mind with reference to some actual incident or anecdote that had come his way, but it is worth remembering that while all sorts of scraps of factual material from a writer's initial conception of a novel may adhere to the completed work, any imaginative creation will reformulate and finally transcend these elements. In *The Secret Agent* Conrad largely invented his *own* apparently unfathomable mystery; he added the special ingredient of Winnie's blind, but intense, maternal love, and then provided a 'solution' to at least two acts of seeming madness and despair.

2.2 ANARCHISM AND THE POLITICAL BACKGROUND

Conrad is not concerned in *The Secret Agent* to offer a critique in ideological terms of the revolutionary characters he portrays; he is more interested in the personal and temperamental motivation of their avowed political allegiance. Nevertheless, it will be useful at this stage to attempt a brief definition of anarchism, as it is one of the main strands of revolutionary thinking that runs through the novel. As an ideology, anarchism is somewhat slippery and amorphous in the content of its ideas, not least because at one extreme it includes in its ranks benignly disposed idealists who are concerned to assert the primacy of the individual against what is seen as the corrupting influence of the state; at the other extreme it embraces the mindless viciousness of the incendiary and the assassin.

A kind of anarchist thinking may be traced back to Zeno, the Ancient Greek Stoic philosopher, but it is probably the French social theorist, Proudhon (1809–65), who formed anarchism into something resembling a coherent movement. In the pamphlet *What is Property?* (1840), Proudhon made his famous assertion that 'property is theft' and, while not advocating violence, he urged all men to emancipate themselves from the scourge of government so they might control their own interests as freely associating individuals rather than as 'slaves'. These ideas merged with a communistic anarchism in the revolutionary ideology of Russians such as Bakunin (1814–76) and Kropotkin (1842–1921): because all authority interfered with personal freedom, the oppressed workers were justified in using any means, including terrorism and assassination, to overthrow the state. There were attempts to unite elements of this 'Bakunist' ideology with Marxism – in 1868 anarchists joined in the First International – but inevitably there was a breach, and anarchism, like much of the whole revolutionary movement, splintered into a number of different groups, the members of which often showed as much antipathy towards each other as they did to the capitalist class. Anarchism essentially rejects the idea of a 'Party'; like Marxism it is opposed to capitalism, but it is equally opposed to the existence of any state or government as such, and to the idea of socialist control as a necessary prelude to a classless society.

Revolution simmered and frequently came to the boil in many parts of Europe throughout the nineteenth century. In the latter decades of the century social discontent was particularly prevalent in Russia under the rule of the Tsars. Of course, everybody looked back, with different feelings, to the French Revolution of 1789. The radical programme associated, for instance, with the abortive attempt of the Commune of Paris in 1871 to assert its authority suggested to European governments – and to their ruling classes and bourgeoisie – that reforms in the franchise or trends towards a measure of liberalisation had not necessarily turned back the tide of revolution. Moreover, to many people the social *status quo* seemed to be particularly precariously balanced because the 1880s and 1890s were generally marked by economic depression.

England, with its political tradition of tolerance, continued to provide a haven for radicals and revolutionaries who fled persecution in their own homelands. Particularly after the assassination (by an anarchist) of Tsar Alexander II in 1881, exiles from Russia grew in numbers. A branch of the Metropolitan Police was made responsible for maintaining surveillance over these exiles, though generally they caused little trouble. The Russian government, however, was rather more interested in them, and it employed secret agents to infiltrate the organisations set up by Russian emigrés and to report on their activities.

This is necessarily a *very* brief account of some aspects of the immediate political background to *The Secret Agent*. It is, of course, just as important to remember that Conrad's own formative years were spent in a Poland dominated by Russia and that his father had been a patriotic and utopian 'revolutionary' who had been sentenced to exile in Russia for his activities.

3 SUMMARIES AND CRITICAL COMMENTARIES

3.1 GENERAL SUMMARY OF THE PLOT

Verloc lives on the premises of his disreputable shop in Soho with his wife, Winnie, her mentally retarded brother, Stevie, and – until she decides to move to an almshouse – his mother-in-law. In fact, the shop is a 'cover' for Verloc's real business: he is a secret agent who reports to a foreign embassy – and to a contact, Chief Inspector Heat, in the British police – on revolutionary and anarchist activity. Vladimir, a new hand at the (Russian) embassy, demands that, if Verloc is to remain in the pay of the embassy, he must take on a more active role as an *agent provocateur*. In order to force the British government into introducing repressive measures against the revolutionaries who find an easy refuge in England, Vladimir demands that popular feeling against them must be whipped up by the planting of a bomb at the Greenwich Observatory. Verloc, who has grown accustomed to his comfortable domestic niche and relatively undemanding employment, is reduced to despair by this proposal, for he knows that the revolutionaries with whom he associates, ineffectual men such as Michaelis, Yundt and Ossipon, are incapable of committing themselves to any concerted action of this kind. As a way out of his dilemma, Verloc trains Stevie to plant the bomb, but the young man botches the job and blows himself up in Greenwich Park. Unbeknown to Verloc, Stevie's coat is labelled with his address – this was sewn there by Winnie to ensure Stevie would not get lost when visiting his mother – and the address tab is found among the remains of the victim's clothing by Chief Inspector Heat after the explosion. Heat would like to adopt his own method of following up the investigation, which is to pin the guilt on Michaelis and to keep secret the very useful connection Heat has maintained with Verloc.

However, Heat's superior, the Assistant Commissioner, is led by certain personal considerations to take a direct hand in the case, and having gained the authority of Sir Ethelred, the Minister of State, to do so, he visits Verloc at the address indicated on the tattered remains of the victim's clothing. On the evening of the day of the explosion, after an interview with Verloc which leads to a full confession, the Assistant Commissioner decides not to arrest the secret agent immediately because he is sure Verloc will not attempt to escape. While the Assistant Commissioner and Verloc are absent from the shop, Heat arrives and in the course of his inquiries he reveals to Winnie the circumstances which have led to Stevie's death.

Winnie, who married Verloc to safeguard her brother's future, is, of course, outraged. Verloc does not appreciate the intensity of his wife's attachment to Stevie and believes that she will finally come to terms with her bereavement. Their whole marriage rests on the inability of each partner to understand one another, or even to communicate properly. In a frenzy of blind passion, Winnie kills her husband. Shortly after the murder Ossipon, one of Verloc's revolutionary associates, arrives on the scene.

Earlier in the day, not long after news of the explosion had been reported, Ossipon had been informed by the Professor, a fiercely malevolent anarchist who will provide virtually anybody who asks with explosives, that he had recently supplied Verloc with a bomb. Not unnaturally, both men have assumed that it must have been Verloc who perished in Greenwich Park. Ossipon's arrival at Verloc's shop that evening is accounted for by his characteristic wish to assess the financial pickings that may be gained from Verloc's widow.

When Ossipon meets the terrified Winnie, she asks him to fly the country with her. Still ignorant of what has really happened to Verloc, Ossipon agrees: they can catch a boat-train to France that evening. However, when Ossipon discovers the true nature of the affair, he feels totally intimidated. He pretends to go through with the plan for flight, extracts from Winnie all the money Verloc had withdrawn from the bank and with which he had entrusted Winnie, but just as the train is drawing out of the station, Ossipon leaps from the carriage and leaves Winnie to her fate. Winnie ends her life by jumping from the night-ferry while it is crossing to France. The novel closes with a broken and guilt-ridden Ossipon offering the Professor the money he has received from Winnie: it will be used to finance the Professor's bomb-making activities.

The above account offers a bare summary of the novel's plot, but it is not the way in which Conrad tells the story. The narrative structure of *The Secret Agent* makes use of switches in time and point of view — most notably perhaps at the beginning of Chapter 8. The notes that follow will attempt to show that these switches, far from being arbitrary or intended simply to puzzle the reader, are integral to the novel's whole purpose and design. In one sense, the way in which the story is told *is* the story. It is hoped that this rather abstract point will be given its concrete demonstration in most of what follows in this guide to the novel.

3.2 CHAPTER SUMMARIES AND COMMENTARIES

Chapter 1

Summary
We are introduced to what is to be the novel's main centre of action, Mr Verloc's seedy premises in Brett Street, Soho where he carries on his 'ostensible business' of retailing material which purports to be pornographic, along with other shoddy, overpriced wares. The shop is frequented during the day by furtive young customers, and it is a meeting place in the evening for mysterious visitors. We meet Verloc and the members of his *ménage* — his wife, Winnie, his mother-in-law, and Stevie, his wife's mentally retarded brother — and we learn that Verloc first met Winnie when he was an occasional guest at the lodging-house maintained by Winnie's mother. In deference to the convenience of Mr Verloc and his 'other business', Winnie's mother has given up running the lodging-house and has moved in with her daughter and son-in-law. The main focus of the lives of Winnie and her mother is to safeguard the future of Stevie.

Commentary
The description of the members of the Verloc household, the shop, its clientele and its immediate surroundings conjures up an impression of a drab, dispiriting existence in which human beings are isolated in their own separate compartments of life. Throughout the novel the evocation of various parts of London in the year 1886 (though it is really the metropolis of the first decade of the twentieth century that Conrad describes) will act as a kind of touchstone to the moral worth of its inhabitants. Conrad strikes the pervasive mood in his 'Author's Note' when he writes of his initial vision of 'an enormous town more populous than some continents . . . a cruel devourer of the world's light. There was room enough there to place any story . . . darkness enough to bury five million lives.'

Concentrating at the outset on one area in this dark metropolis, Verloc's shop in Soho, right from the novel's opening page Conrad cleverly insinuates the idea that appearances are not to be accepted at face value. Verloc's shop is obviously a 'front' for some more secret activities, and Conrad tantalisingly hints at what Verloc's 'other business' may entail: there are, for instance, references to Verloc's vague explanation to Winnie that 'his work was in a way political' and we learn that after returning home in the early hours, his voice the next morning sounded like that of 'a man who had been talking vehemently for many hours together'. However, the notion of Verloc doing anything 'vehemently' may strike the reader as an incongruous idea, for the opening portrait of Verloc presents us with a man who, while obviously leading a secret life, seems to be lethargically dedicated to pursuing domestic ease and routine. His wife, Winnie, also appears to be impassive and uncommunicative, yet there are hints of a repressed sensuality – for example, in the description of her 'full bust, in a tight bodice' – and, like her mother, Winnie is obviously fired by a strong protective passion towards her brother, Stevie.

Stevie's 'stroke of originality' – his misconceived pyrotechnical display on his employer's premises – offers a grim foreshadowing of later, fatal activities, and it demonstrates that, while Stevie is a simpleton, his powerful, yet incoherent, feelings of compassion towards the suffering of the oppressed are very strong; Stevie is impressionable and easily manipulated. Already Conrad is pointing up certain ambiguities and contradictions in the situation described, and once the reader knows the whole novel he will return to Chapter 1 and see how skilfully Conrad has woven a whole web of ironies which were initially only barely visible. (If you are uncertain about what is meant by irony, turn to p.76 for a definition.) Most obviously, the pathetic faith of Winnie's mother in Verloc's 'kind and generous disposition' to Stevie will ring hollow later in the novel, as will the whole notion that Verloc is some kind of insouciant benefactor. In a more subtle fashion we shall certainly wish to question the perception Verloc nurtures of himself as one who 'exercised his vocation of a protector of society and cultivated his domestic virtues'. We shall discover that Verloc is more of a parasite than a protector of society, and as for the practice of his 'domestic virtues' – how oddly this claim sorts with some of the wares in his shop – that part of his life will be shown to rest on a massive failure to comprehend that his whole marriage is a tacit lie.

Most importantly in this opening chapter, Conrad establishes the credentials of his narrator. Clearly the author of this story knows much more than he is yet prepared to tell. The tone he adopts suggests that the narrative will unfold at the pace he chooses and that he will maintain a magisterial distance from the characters he creates. For instance, the narrator's contempt for Verloc is immediately apparent in the introduction to this character: the tone is one of amused ironic detachment blended with punctilious disdain. (For a fuller discussion of the role of Conrad's narrator, see p.78.)

Chapter 2

Summary
Neatly dressed for some obviously important meeting and in a complacently benevolent mood, Verloc leaves his shop and, after passing westwards through the more affluent parts of the metropolis, he finally arrives at his destination – an embassy. In a preliminary interview with Privy Councillor Wurmt it becomes clear to the reader that Verloc has been employed for some years as a spy by the authorities at the embassy – a thinly disguised version of the Russian embassy – and that Verloc's role is to report on the revolutionary organisations he has infiltrated. Wurmt emphasises to Verloc that a more active effort will be required of him: Wurmt's government considers that the British police and the courts are far too lenient in their treatment of the revolutionaries who have found refuge in England. Verloc is ushered into the presence of Vladimir, the First Secretary, who begins by abusing Verloc for his alleged inactivity and brushing aside Verloc's attempts to justify his record of service. Life for the embassy spy will not be as undemanding as it has been under the previous regime of His Excellency Baron Stott-Wartenheim, for Vladimir assures Verloc that in future he must *earn* his pay as an *agent provocateur*. Having lectured Verloc on the mechanics of influencing political decision-making by Machiavellian methods, the First Secretary, to Verloc's horror, reveals the reason why the secret agent has been summoned and unfolds the plan which Verloc must put into action: within a month Verloc must arrange for a bomb to be planted at the Greenwich Observatory. Vladimir believes that an outrage of this kind, aimed with what will strike the popular imagination as an unfathomable violence directed at science, one of society's sacred cows, will shock the English bourgeoisie into demanding that their political masters introduce repressive measures against the revolutionaries for whom at present the nation provides a sanctuary. Such an outrage, Vladimir calculates, will also influence the deliberations of an international conference which is currently considering what action should be taken to suppress political crime.

Verloc returns home in a state of total desperation. His taciturn stupor makes Winnie and her mother particularly anxious to ensure that Stevie should not offend Verloc, the young man's providential saviour.

Commentary
This chapter slowly unfolds and clarifies the nature of Verloc's real 'business' which lies behind the façade of his disreputable shop in Soho, and it provides the impetus for the whole action of the novel. The self-satisfied, paternal outlook towards the people Verloc believes he 'protects' – the dominant note of the opening of the chapter – will soon strike the reader as being highly ironic. In fact, as Verloc crosses London, unbeknown to him, he is walking towards a crisis which will sow the seeds of anarchic violence; moreover, in the short term, it is a crisis which will undermine the whole comfortable and even tenor of his domestic routine.

Vladimir's words and whole manner are cleverly calculated to erode Verloc's self-confidence – this includes taunts about the secret agent's corpulence and life-style of bourgeois respectability – and to wound his complacent pride in his function as a spy, for as the opening of the chapter makes clear, Verloc does have a high estimate of his professional value to the public at large. Yet at bottom, the truly threatening nature of the challenge, couched in Vladimir's terse formula of 'No work, no pay', is the jeopardising of Verloc's comfortable niche as an embassy spy. Verloc's deepest temperamental needs have been satisfied by an existence in which the repose of his domestic life is securely supported by a relatively undemanding kind of vocation. The next part of the narrative will see Verloc wrestling with the problem Vladimir sets him with increasing desperation. Verloc's botched solution then sets up a sequence of events which, at the end of the novel, will lead to a similar seismic disturbance in two other lives. The chain of cause and effect goes right back to Vladimir's bizarre scheme outlined in Chapter 2. (For a discussion of Conrad's attitude to Vladimir, see p.72.)

The effect of the description of the scenes on the London streets is once again noteworthy. The atmosphere changes from the dinginess of Soho, but there remains a sense of lives lived in separate compartments; we are given fleeting glimpses of other existences – as, for instance, when a carriage passes 'with the skin of some wild beast inside and a woman's face and hat emerging above the folded hood' – and they carry recurring suggestions of the randomness of life in the city, along with an impression of its barely suppressed violence and cruelty. Objects often take on a strange, dream-like quality – a policeman looks 'a stranger to every emotion, as if he, too, were part of inorganic nature, surging apparently out of a lamp-post' – and the hazy scene at the opening of the chapter, with its blotches and gleams of colour and diffused light, suggests that external reality may be no more than the arrangement which the individual mind imposes on it. Yet objects, 'inorganic nature', do possess a permanence which is beyond man; reality exhibits also an irreducible quirkiness, as we see, for instance, in the inscrutable system for the numbering of houses in Chesham Square. Description of this kind produces a disturbing undertone which sounds ironically behind Verloc's complacent mood as he walks towards the embassy; it forms an appropriate prelude to a confrontation which will commit Verloc to a world of uncertainty. Moreover, the impressions we have recorded of the scenes on the London streets act as a mirror for one of Conrad's central preoccupations in the novel: Conrad will show us that what we complacently assume to be a fixed reality invariably slides away from our pattern-making attempts to impose meaning and order on it.

The last part of the chapter sheds more light on the uncommunicative Winnie. We learn that before she married Verloc she was courted by 'a steady young fellow, only son of a butcher in the next street', but she obviously made a decision to suppress any idea of romantic fulfilment: marriage to Mr Verloc seemed to provide a better insurance policy for Stevie's future. But this chapter has already initiated a series of events which will destroy the reality Winnie imagines she has constructed for Stevie and herself.

Chapter 3

Summary
In Verloc's parlour behind the shop, Verloc listens dispiritedly to what are clearly the over-familiar arguments of three of his revolutionary associates. Each of the three men, the grotesquely obese Michaelis, the violently disposed but decrepitly impotent Yundt, and Ossipon, a parasitic womaniser and a failed medical student, rides the hobbyhorse of his personal revolutionary ideology. Michaelis believes that economic forces are predestined to bring about the millennium of socialism; Yundt sadistically advocates that the most extreme forms of violence against a corrupt society are justified; Ossipon, who edits anarchist pamphlets, airs his views which derive from Lombroso (1836–1909), an Italian criminologist whose theories asserted that criminal types could be detected from their physical features. The violent rhetoric, which includes Yundt's imagery of cannibalism and

retribution, triggers a powerful emotional response in Stevie, who overhears these tirades.

When his colleagues depart, Verloc reflects despairingly on their ineffectuality; he cannot expect any assistance from them in lifting from his shoulders the burden that Vladimir has placed there. Verloc feels totally isolated; he faces a dark impasse. His career as a secret agent seems doomed, and he reflects that the proceeds from the shop alone were never intended to support the domestic ease to which he is accustomed – or the responsibilities of a family which, almost without being fully aware of them, he has taken on.

To meet the practical demands of getting the still highly excited Stevie to bed, Verloc has to rouse Winnie. Later, as he undresses for bed, Verloc is plainly facing another night of insomnia and he is at one point almost on the verge of disclosing his apparently hopeless situation to Winnie, but his wife is preoccupied with explanations and excuses for Stevie's behaviour. The moment passes.

Commentary

We are to imagine that Verloc has spent many similar evenings listening to the blathering of men such as Michaelis, Yundt and Ossipon. Previously this has been, no doubt, a tedious yet relatively painless chore, Verloc's main task being to single out any items of information which he may, for his own advantage, pass on to his employers at the embassy or even to his contact in the police. But now we look through Verloc's eyes at these windbag associates with a view to their potential as men of action who may assist Verloc in furthering Vladimir's plan. There is, of course, no hope. In his portrayal of the revolutionary characters Conrad certainly puts his finger in the balance to tip the scale against them. They are, in various ways, physically repellent; moreover, they are shown to be lazy parasites who are widely separated on fundamental matters of belief; they are preoccupied with jargon-ridden talk rather than positive action and motivated largely by personal weakness and inadequacy. These are the men on whom Verloc spends his life keeping a careful watch so that society may be protected; these are the revolutionaries from whom, according to Vladimir, so much is to be feared. It is not surprising that, mesmerised by the ever-present mental spectre of Vladimir, Verloc 'was not satisfied with his friends. In the light of Mr. Vladimir's philosophy of bomb throwing they appeared hopelessly futile.'

Ironically, it is only Stevie who is persuasively affected by the proceedings in Verloc's parlour. Winnie is made to develop this irony in a way she cannot, of course, appreciate when, in defence of Stevie, she remarks to her husband: 'That boy hears too much of what is talked about here. . . He believes it's all true. He knows no better.' She also reports to her husband that after her brother had read one of Ossipon's pamphlets which contained a particularly brutal story of a German officer tearing the ear of a recruit half-off – yet another image of mutilated, branded or even metaphorically cannibalised flesh of the kind that runs through the chapter – she had to take the carving knife from the boy (yet another foreshadowing irony): 'He would have stuck that officer like a pig if he had seen him then.' The fact that Stevie is so simple-mindedly impressionable and easily aroused by images of cruelty and human suffering will be of crucial importance later in the novel. In one sense, Stevie is the ideal subject for propaganda. Moreover, as Winnie will constantly impress upon her husband, Stevie is capable of absolute devotion and loyalty. This lad, despised or ignored by the revolutionaries who frequent Verloc's parlour, in fact possesses the makings of the perfect anarchist instrument. At present, those strong feelings, which make the theoretical disputes we have witnessed look like so much shadow-boxing, have no real target. Stevie's obsessive drawing of circles suggests a maimed, imprisoned rationality searching for the simplicity of perfect order, but reduced to the creation of chaos and incoherent repetition. When Verloc is made to realise what special potential Stevie possesses, it will appear to Verloc as though his brother-in-law has been purpose-built to perform an act which is beyond the compass of even the most extreme of his usual circle of revolutionary associates.

The seed of the realisation of Stevie's potential usefulness to Verloc is, unbeknown to both Winnie and Verloc, being planted even as, at the end of the chapter, Winnie makes her apologia on her brother's behalf. However, it is conceivable, for a moment, that events might have taken a different turn with Verloc making a clean breast to his wife of his problem. It could be argued that it is principally Winnie's characteristic preoccupation with Stevie that, at the end of the chapter, distracts her from making any attempt to examine more closely her husband's declaration that he is feeling unwell; but Winnie is constitutionally disinclined, as Conrad will endlessly remind us, 'to look beneath the surface of things'. For Verloc to open his heart to his wife would go against the whole grain of their marriage, which has always been based on an astonishing capacity for non-communication. The final words of the chapter, which record the turning off of the light in the Verlocs' bedroom, symbolises, as is also the case at the end of Chapter 8, the elimination of any possibility of Verloc's sharing his waking nightmare with his wife.

Chapter 4

Summary
In a beer-cellar, the Silenus, Ossipon is in conversation with the Professor, a puny, unprepossessing man who is, nevertheless, an anarchist *par excellence* whose life is streamlined to the pure function of developing the perfect detonator and to supplying explosives to virtually anybody who requires them. The Professor is, quite literally, a 'walking bomb', for, as a disincentive to any policeman who may wish to arrest him, he carries on his own person an explosive device which he can detonate at will.

We gradually realise that the time sequence of the novel has moved on: a month has elapsed since the end of Chapter 3. Ossipon has just read a newspaper report concerning an unnamed victim of a bomb explosion in Greenwich Park, and he presses the Professor for information. The Professor is at first uncommunicative, but much to Ossipon's astonishment he does finally reveal that he recently supplied Verloc with a bomb. Both men naturally draw the conclusion that some accident must have caused Verloc to meet his death in Greenwich Park. Ossipon regards maverick activities of this kind as an unwarrantable endangering of the position of the revolutionary cause – and of his own source of income as editor of his propagandist pamphlets – and he decides that his party of revolutionaries must dissociate themselves from any connection with the abortive bomb attack. He wonders whether it will be safe for him to visit Verloc's shop in order to find out more information. The Professor, obviously alluding to Ossipon's parasitic way with susceptible women, wryly advises him to fasten upon Winnie Verloc.

Commentary
The surprising shift in time and point of view in this chapter creates suspense; one character is asking another, who is at first uncommunicative, for information. All that Ossipon knows about Verloc, whom we see from a new perspective, makes it hard for him to believe that Verloc would attempt to plant a bomb at this particular time, but then the evidence supplied by the Professor seems to allow for no other view of the affair. The reader, too, who has witnessed at first hand Verloc's wrestling with the task imposed upon him by Vladimir, may also be inclined to accept the hypothesis that the secret agent, in despair at the passive incompetence of his revolutionary associates, has been driven to plant the bomb himself and has met an untimely death.

In the next part of the narrative, the uncovering of what actually took place in Greenwich Park, and the events that led up to the explosion, will provide an element of 'detective story' interest; the narrator will supply a number of hints and clues which make us question Ossipon's view of the affair. However, what principally interests Conrad is the general idea of the relativity of truth. The 'truth' in *The Secret Agent* is rarely simple. Characters in the novel are invariably in possession of only a part of the truth or a distorted version of it, and this is one reason why their actions habitually produce unforeseen, or even counter-productive and bizarre outcomes. The way in which Conrad structures the novel at this point places the *reader* in a position of partial knowledge and probably nudges him or her into speculating that, of course, it must have been Verloc who blew himself up in Greenwich Park.

The narrative has in one sense placed the reader in the privileged position of knowing much more than Ossipon. We can recognise many of the limitations of Ossipon's point of view: for instance, we can see the superficiality of many of Ossipon's opinions about Verloc; Ossipon has never questioned why Verloc so successfully eludes the attention of the police, and Ossipon actually believes that the shop in Soho is run on a sound economic basis. It may be that our sense of Verloc's characteristic inertia makes us question the image of him as an active, if inept, planter of bombs, but when we take into account the factor of which Ossipon, of course, can have no knowledge – that is, what appears to Verloc as the intolerable pressure Vladimir has brought to bear on him – it is likely that we begin to form the kind of mistaken hypothesis noted above. In fact, the narrator has played a kind of trick on us; we have been placed in a position analogous to that of one of the characters in the novel; later discoveries will show that we really know much less than we think we do.

Structurally, this chapter marks the end of what we might term the exposition of the novel and begins a loop of time which will see Ossipon returning to the narrative in Chapter 12 when he arrives at Verloc's shop. (Significantly, in the final chapter, the narrative will come to rest in this same scene, with another newspaper report in front of Ossipon which will describe a second fatality, though in this case Ossipon will be directly implicated.) Ossipon has been placed in a situation which has some parallels with that of Verloc after his interview with Vladimir. The pressure on Ossipon is not as intense as that experienced by Verloc, but Ossipon's feelings register that 'the even tenor of his revolutionary life was menaced by no fault of his', and he experiences a similar sense of anxiety and loss of bearings. Acting just as Verloc does, he will constitutionally follow the line of least resistance. Yet his almost instinctive leechlike inclination to seek out Winnie Verloc – he does not really need the Professor's advice to move in this direction – will have dire repercussions for Ossipon which he cannot possibly envisage.

The chapter ends with another description of the streets outside the Silenus. A familiar litany of key words – 'gloomy', 'grimy', 'damp', 'soiled' and 'filth' – evokes the pervasive atmosphere of London.

Chapter 5

Summary
We see the Professor on his way home from the Silenus. He is disappointed by what he takes to be Verloc's failure, though he attempts to reassure himself that next time the really telling blow of terror will be delivered against the society he hates. He encounters by chance Chief Inspector Heat, a police officer whose special responsibility is to organise the surveillance of revolutionary activity in the metropolis. After a mere couple of exchanges, the narrator takes us back through the events of Heat's unsatisfactory day, as seen from the Inspector's standpoint. The explosion that took place in Greenwich Park is particularly annoying to Heat because only a few days earlier he had given an assurance to a 'high official' that there was no possibility of any anarchist activities taking place in the immediate future. And Heat prides himself on his status as an expert in anarchist procedure. We learn that Heat was called to Greenwich Park shortly after the explosion occurred and later in a mortuary he examined the remains of the dismembered corpse of a slight, fair man which a policeman had collected together. Heat is informed that a witness saw two men coming out of the local station – one large, the other fair and thin – and that the men were carrying what appeared to be a 'tin varnish can'. It is assumed that the victim of the explosion must have stumbled over some tree roots, thus detonating the bomb prematurely. Heat pockets a strip of cloth which he has torn from the velvet collar of the dead man's coat. This is clearly a valuable piece of evidence, and – for reasons as yet undisclosed – the idea forms in Heat's mind that it will probably be desirable to keep secret the identity of the bomb-carrying victim.

Although Heat has conducted himself with his usual official aplomb, it has nevertheless been a harrowing day and he is not really in the mood to confront the Professor who is well-known to the Inspector – as is the presence of the anarchist's 'pocket bomb'. Heat understands thieves: they recognise virtually the same moral conventions as policemen; but the mentality of anarchists Heat finds largely inscrutable. The Inspector dismisses the Professor's taunts with the response that when the right time comes the anarchist's days of pestilential freedom will be over, and he then continues his journey, the purpose of which is to make a report on his investigation to his relatively new superior, the Assistant Commissioner. Heat is wary of his superior because he suspects that the Assistant Commissioner is likely to interfere with the investigation into the Greenwich Park explosion which Heat would like to follow up in his own way. In fact, it is made clear in their discussion of the case that the Assistant Commissioner is distrustful of Heat's 'old hand' methods, though he has some respect for the Inspector's past record of service, and something of a battle of wits develops between the two men. The Assistant Commissioner is obviously somewhat bored by his desk-bound role and the lack of opportunity it affords for real detective work; his interest in Heat's very guarded account of his investigations is suddenly and strongly aroused when the Inspector mentions it is known that Michaelis is staying at a cottage near the country station from which the two men carrying the bomb travelled.

Commentary
The opening of the chapter provides us with more background information about the Professor and confirms our impression that the fanatical nature of his anarchism rests on a highly developed sense of personal grievance. Because society has not recognised his talents in the way he imagines he deserves, society must be made to pay the price. Conrad emphasises throughout the novel that a political ideology grows out of a character's constitutional nature – his strengths and weaknesses of temperament; it is Conrad's jaundiced diagnosis of the revolutionary mentality in *The Secret Agent* that it grows principally out of weaknesses of character.(This point is discussed further on p.69.) 'Lost in the crowd, miserable and undersized,' the Professor from this perspective does not now seem anything like the frightening prospect he appeared to be when he so contemptuously intimidated Ossipon in the Silenus. The Professor's ferocious vanity is more likely to strike us now as a form of mental derangement. It is by means of changes of perspective of this kind that Conrad achieves many of his most characteristic effects of narration. The Professor may embody that most perfect form of moral anarchism – a will to destroy which includes even self-destruction – but he is daunted by the endless crowds that pass him by, heedless of his self-appointed, avenging mission. In moments of doubt he is made to feel that the amorphous mass of mankind may be impervious even to his final weapon of terror.

In contrast, Heat feels the reassuring support of the majority of humanity on his side in his official function, which is to contain and destroy the forces of revolution, but here also Conrad's irony sceptically questions Heat's role. It is clear that the world of the police and that of the criminal interpenetrate in many ways; Heat is perfectly at home with the mentality of thieves. Moreover, while Heat may indulge in a little breastbeating as an official who has 'an authorised mission on earth' – a tendency we observed earlier in no less a person than Verloc – the main practical direction of his thoughts is centred on a kind of inter-departmental struggle that is being conducted between himself and his superior. Heat wishes to preserve his own autonomy of action; he regards the relatively new Assistant Commissioner as an interfering amateur, a meddler in highly complex matters which should be left to experts; he is engaged in playing an intricate game which rests on his personal judgment – disguised perhaps as what would be best for the Department – of what facts should come to light and who should be made to carry the responsibility for the bomb outrage. Already, for instance, he has decided for reasons that will be made clear later – they centre on the usefulness to him of Verloc's past services as an informant – that it would be best if the identity of the victim of the bomb remained undisclosed.

The most significant technical feature of the chapter is the shift in time which Conrad introduces almost immediately after the Professor encounters Heat in the decaying alley. There will be a similar interlude at the beginning of the next chapter which explains the Assistant Commissioner's sudden arousal of interest at the mention of Michaelis's name. The purpose of some of these switches in time may not be immediately apparent to the reader, but already the narrator has established his credentials as an artificer who is engaged in a painstaking piecing together of the many strands of a complex pattern of events. Conrad the novelist *is* an 'investigating animal' – unlike most of the characters in the novel – and to understand reactions in the present he knows that they invariably need to be placed in the context of explanations which derive from the past. So, although the reader may initially be puzzled by some of the switches in the novel's time-scheme, he accepts that at some point these causal relationships which move in various sequences of time will click together in an enlightening manner. Time itself is, in fact, an important idea in the novel which will be discussed later (see p.62).

The narrator's tone in this chapter is often at its most mordant. We are not spared, for instance, the gruesome details of the dismembered corpse which the police constable scrapes together. Earlier images of torn and – in figurative terms – cannibalised flesh achieve a kind of grotesque acme as the mangled remains are described as 'what might have been an accumulation of raw material for a cannibal feast' or as Heat's peering at the remains on the table in the mortuary is likened to 'the slightly anxious attention of an indigent customer bending over what may be called the by-products of a butcher's shop with a view to an inexpensive Sunday dinner'. This is black humour of a high order in which the punctilious precision of diction, syntax and metaphor produces a queasy spasm. Yet the final effect is to reduce human flesh to mere material and to distance the reader from a direct emotional response to the horror of the victim's fate.

Chapter 6

Summary
An elderly, aristocratic lady who invites to her salons an oddly assorted mixture of figures of the day – she likes to imagine that she keeps her finger on the pulse of the age – has adopted Michaelis as a protégé. Indeed, it is she who has provided Michaelis with a cottage in the country where he is currently writing his autobiography. The lady's social prejudices are attracted by many of the ideas Michaelis has expounded to her. The Assistant Commissioner is also admitted to this lady's social circle, as is his wife, and the connection between this lady of high society and the Assistant Commissioner's rather tiresome wife is one which he is most anxious to preserve. He recognises that if he allows Heat to incriminate Michaelis in investigations into the Greenwich affair, Michaelis's 'ticket-of-leave' will be cancelled and he will finish his days in prison. The Assistant Commissioner knows that Michaelis's patroness would hold him personally responsible for such an eventuality and that this would terminate the desirable connection between the lady and his wife.

After the reason for the Assistant Commissioner's personal interest in the fate of Michaelis has been established, the narrative returns to the interview between the Assistant Commissioner and Chief Inspector Heat. Heat's complacent assertions that Michaelis is the man to be made publicly accountable for the Greenwich affair goad the Assistant Commissioner to bring his considerable skills as a detective to bear on his Chief Inspector. Almost intuitively, he senses that Heat is hiding something from him, and he presses this accusation, much to Heat's chagrin. The Inspector has been accustomed to his superiors gratefully taking on trust his suggestions concerning the direction that enquiries of this kind should follow: he likes to develop his own strategies and rules. Heat had clearly at one stage been intending to suppress the evidence of the piece of cloth salvaged from the dead man's collar – it bears the address of Verloc's premises in Soho – and to follow his own discrete investigation, but though his superior's approach seems to him inept and unprofessional, he decides that there is no alternative but to follow a more open policy. The production of the address tab leads the Assistant Commissioner to elicit from Heat the nature of Verloc's position as an embassy spy and as an informant upon whom rests much of Heat's success as an investigator in the Special Crimes branch. At the end of the chapter, we see the Assistant Commissioner, with some sense of liberation, poised to take the control of investigations into his own hands.

Commentary
As the police enquiry gets under way, so begins the process which will reveal the events that led up to the explosion in Greenwich Park and who was involved in the affair, but it is a freakish birth for the delivery of truth. Conrad's amused irony directs the reader's attention to the way in which neither of the two policemen is concerned with the disinterested pursuit of truth as an overriding priority. Heat, for instance, is fairly sure that Michaelis played, at best, only a peripheral part in the Greenwich affair, but he is quite prepared to suppress evidence and to present Michaelis as a sacrificial offering should an outraged press and public opinion require a head on a platter. He knows bigger fish are involved, but for a number of essentially self-interested reasons, he is not prepared at this juncture to angle for them. The vital piece of evidence which he reluctantly produces for the Assistant Commissioner points directly to Verloc's involvement, and behind Verloc looms the possibility that a foreign embassy has some insidious connection with the whole affair. Yet Heat blandly asserts that he feels sure Verloc 'knows nothing of this affair'. In one sense, Heat is basing his judgment on what he knows of Verloc: the secret agent, 'a lazy dog', is hardly the stuff of which the planters of bombs are made. Heat's view of Verloc presents us with yet another perspective from which he may be viewed; it is one which is based on certain preconceptions and, of course, on complete ignorance of the intolerable pressure (intolerable for Verloc) which has been applied to the secret agent to make him act in an uncharacteristic manner. However, the real spring of Heat's whole approach is a desire to protect the secrecy of what has obviously been a very useful source of information. The irony is that Verloc's activities have supported not only his own domestic ease, but much of the Chief Inspector's investigative success and prestige.

Throughout this chapter, and indeed the whole novel, a consideration of what may, or may not, be regarded as belonging exclusively to the private or public domain forms a strong undercurrent. We will note, for example, the fraudulence of Heat's insistence that his relations with Verloc are an entirely *private* matter. The realisation that the private and public concern may not always be kept in discrete compartments has already been forced painfully on Verloc. The more sophisticated Assistant Commissioner knows already that it is not tenable to claim that 'private' concerns do not influence a man's actions in an official capacity. For what is it that provides the motive force for the Assistant Commissioner's desire to discover the nature of the devious game Heat is playing and the suppressions of information that result? The answer is, of course, found in the background details which the narrator has provided in the first part of the chapter; the reader's knowledge of the nature of the Assistant Commissioner's relationship with Michaelis's patroness and his desire to maintain a *modus vivendi* which requires that his wife should be 'kept happy', makes it abundantly clear that the Assistant Commissioner is quite the equal of his Chief Inspector in terms of following self-serving motives. The Assistant Commissioner may be sardonically aware of his motives in wishing to keep Michaelis out of Heat's hands, but these motives are powerfully operative; ironically, when allied with the Assistant Commissioner's considerable intelligence, the line dictated by expediency will push him in the right direction. Other factors, too, make him eager to escape the stultifying routines of his desk-bound role and to engage in some 'real' detective work as a lone wolf: a desire to challenge his Chief Inspector's *modus operandi* has been simmering for some time; the Assistant Commissioner is temperamentally suspicious of the standard methods of police procedure. Yet, if the name of Michaelis had not cropped up in Heat's report, it is unlikely that the Assistant Commissioner would have taken the particularly active role we will see him adopting to track down the 'truth' of the Greenwich affair.

Throughout the novel, Conrad is eager to draw our attention to the strange, apparently almost casual way in which the links of causal connection are forged. The reader will be shown that there is a reason for everything that happens in the narrative, although invariably it lies buried in the self-interest and blindness of Conrad's characters. Conrad's deeply sceptical mind structures the novel in such a way as to allow us to see a world in which apparently random events and human motivations click together to create a peculiar destiny for characters who are invariably powerless to perceive or to control their fate. The fact that the reader is given a privileged position denied the characters is the source of Conrad's richest ironies; the reader is invited to share the author's own blend of lofty scorn – and a degree of pity – towards his creations. This outlook operates in terms of even the smallest details in the novel. For instance, Conrad directs us to note with his own amused detachment the vagaries of public opinion as manipulated by the popular press – a complete *volte face* has occurred in the public's attitude to Michaelis – or to observe wryly the myopia of Michaelis's patroness, whose prejudices against the bourgeoisie lead her to find Michaelis's vision of the socialist future very attractive, while she regard her own interests and position as invulnerable to even the direst social cataclysm.

Chapter 7

Summary
The Assistant Commissioner secures an interview with the Secretary of State (presumably for Home Affairs) who is initially somewhat ill-disposed towards the Special Crimes branch as a result of Heat's erroneous assurance which had ruled out the possibility of any immediate anarchist activities in London. The Secretary of State, Sir Ethelred, is also very preoccupied with pressing parliamentary affairs, but he grants the Assistant Commissioner a limited, specified time to outline the bare essentials of his business, and the great man's interest is quickly aroused by the account of the wider ramifications of the Greenwich explosion which involve the strong suspicion that a foreign embassy has employed an *agent provocateur*. The Assistant Commissioner stresses that the investigation will require careful direction and, because of its wide and sensitive political implications, he asks Sir Ethelred to agree to his taking the entire conduct of the case into his own hands. He asserts that Heat's approach would simply follow the short-sighted aim of using the case to lock up as many anarchists as possible on the strength of flimsy evidence. The Assistant Commissioner also asks for the authority to guarantee Verloc's safety in return for information about those who instigated the explosion. Sir Ethelred agrees to these proposals, and the Assistant Commissioner promises to return as soon as possible with a report of what he has discovered after visiting Verloc's premises at Brett Street.

After a short conversation with Toodles, Sir Ethelred's secretary, in which the Assistant Commissioner is informed of the strain the great man is under as he strives to get his bill for the nationalisation of fisheries through Parliament, the Assistant Commissioner returns to his office and, with considerable relish, disguises himself with a few elementary touches which give him a certain 'foreign' appearance. With a sense of excitement and liberation in re-assuming the role of the practising detective in pursuit of his prey, he arrives, after a meal in an Italian restaurant, at a grimy and darkly brooding Brett Street.

Commentary
The novel abounds in discussion, interviews and confrontations which involve two people, and as the pairings switch, perspectives, of course, alter. In this chapter we see the remorselessly clinical intimidator of Heat adopting a role – urbane, deferential, but in fact deeply manipulative – which is precisely calculated to create a good impression with his superior in order to achieve the Assistant Commissioner's self-serving ends. Of course, he justifies the desirability of his assuming complete control of the investigation in terms of a carefully argued appeal to political and tactical issues. The reader, however, is aware of the true perspective, and when Sir Ethelred asks 'But what first put you in motion in this direction?' the reader will recognise that the Assistant Commissioner is necessarily disingenuous when he puts it all down to 'a new man's antagonism to old methods'. At the same time, although the Assistant Commissioner has really been prompted to action by the premise that, if at all possible, Michaelis must be kept out of the affair, we will admire the Assistant Commissioner's perception, which has already brought him close to many of the important elements of the case – though even he can have, as yet, no conception of the truly staggering essential motivation behind Verloc's actions.

An earlier reference will already have alerted the reader to note that the victim of the explosion was slight and fair; now the Assistant Commissioner underlines the details of the 'peculiar stupidity and feebleness in the conduct of the affair' and the curious facts that the victim seems to have been led to the spot in Greenwich Park as though he were some 'deaf mute' and that his coat was labelled with his address. These observations will all support the reader's increasingly strong supposition that the unfortunate individual whose mangled remains were scattered around an area of Greenwich Park must be no other than poor Stevie. This element of 'detective story' interest places the reader in the pleasurable position of working out and testing his own hypothesis. However, at the end of this chapter, just at the moment when Conrad has aroused our expectations, with the 'detective' assuming a disguise and on the point of interviewing *the* vital suspect, Conrad will tantalise the reader: when we expect to learn almost immediately about the outcome of the Assistant Commissioner's visit to Verloc's shop, the conventional chronological order of the narrative is dislocated and we move *backwards* in time instead of forwards.

Conrad's attitude to Sir Ethelred is essentially satirical, though in a playfully mocking way. The main source of the satire is Sir Ethelred's self-interestedly distorted priorities. (This aspect of his character is discussed on p.72.) It is likely that we should also be distrustful of Sir Ethelred because of his insistence, expressed in what virtually becomes a catchphrase, that events be presented to him in the shortest possible time, and in the form of a summary of a few essential facts. Do we not find here yet another example of the simplifying tendency so characteristic of nearly all the characters in the novel? The 'facts' that interest Conrad cannot be presented in the form of a short check-list. The whole structure of *The Secret Agent* affirms that an approach to truth may be made only through the slow drawing together of numerous facts, which trail behind them feelings, prejudices, instincts, misunderstandings, and so on, and a painstaking appreciation of their unique combination. As if almost to frustrate the glib requirements of those who, like Sir Ethelred, require a quick précis of human affairs, the next part of the narrative will, as was noted above, follow the logic of the Conradian mode of investigation through an extended shift in time.

Chapter 8

Summary
The narrator moves the focus back to the Verloc *ménage*, and the reader gradually realises that the time-scheme of the novel has also shifted back to the period some weeks *before* the explosion at Greenwich Park, the planning of which obviously remains a problem which reduces Verloc to a brooding state of taciturn despair.

Winnie's mother has decided that it will be much to Stevie's advantage if she no longer lives with her daughter and son-in-law. Her selfless motives, which Winnie in her peevish surprise virtually completely fails to appreciate, derive from a wish to safeguard Stevie's future. She feels that to continue in residence at Brett Street may put a strain on the good nature of her son-in-law; moreover, by moving away she hopes to ensure that, when she dies, Stevie's complete dependence on Mr Verloc will be a *fait accompli*. Therefore, with some deviousness, but with a kind of heroic self-denial, Winnie's mother has arranged to live in a charity almshouse run for destitute widows, to which new accommodation Winnie and Stevie accompany her. During the journey through a funereal London in a hackney carriage, Stevie is driven into a highly excited state when the cab driver urges on the emaciated horse with his whip, and Stevie causes some consternation by jumping down from the carriage as though to ease the horse's burden. Stevie is ever sensitive to the sufferings of the downtrodden; however, when the cabman points out that his own impoverished life is not an easy one – he works through the night and has to accept whatever horse his employers give him, for he has a wife and four children to support – Stevie's mind is incapable of grasping the full complexity of the factors involved in the situation, the solution of which is beyond his violent, impotent rage and simple desire for retribution.

After Winnie has arrived with her mother at her cramped, miserable dwelling, she informs her mother that she need have no anxiety that Stevie will get lost when, in future, he crosses London to visit the almshouse. (In fact, we will learn later that the solution to this problem involves labelling Stevie's coat with his address.) As Winnie accompanies Stevie home to Brett Street, it is clear that she has no conception of the reasons for Stevie's highly-wrought emotional state.

Later that evening, in the Verloc's bedroom, Winnie is preoccupied with how she and Stevie will come to terms with their mother's absence. A temperamental desire not to look beneath the surface of things ensures that she does not take up her husband's cryptic comment that perhaps her mother's departure is 'for the best'. For his part, Verloc is once again almost on the point of making a clean breast to his wife of the apparently insuperable problem he is facing, but a combination of timidity, natural indolence and an essential affection for Winnie – in so far as his wife epitomises his proprietary ideal of a domestic peace which is now so threatened – makes Verloc abandon the idea. Instead, he informs her that he plans to go the continent for a week or perhaps a fortnight.

Commentary
The shift in narrative focus and time-sequence which occurs in this chapter may seem initially to be a tangential one, but, in fact, it is central to Conrad's thematic and structural concerns in *The Secret Agent*. It grows out of the 'ironic treatment' which in his 'Author's Note' Conrad states he was determined to apply to the events and characters in the novel. The general nature of Conrad's irony will be discussed later (see p.76), but at this point it is worth noting the extent to which irony in the novel underlines the idea of 'purposes gone astray'. Winnie's mother's decision to move to the almshouse is one of the few altruistic actions we witness in the novel. In one sense her life effectively is about to end at this point: the suggestions are

there in the description of the 'Cab of Death' which carries her to her coffin-like dwelling. But though she is prepared to sacrifice her own life for the good of Stevie, the repercussions of her decision to move from Brett Street are entirely counter-productive to her aims. In her mother's absence, we shall see Winnie in the following chapter encouraging her husband to take a more personal interest in Stevie; the holiday break in Michaelis's cottage is no doubt seen by her as something that will lift Stevie's spirits after their mother's departure; she will, moreover, impress on her husband the young man's docility and loyalty. Without knowing it, Winnie is handing over the cherished Stevie to his destroyer.

Another of these curious causal links leads us to the awareness that in an indirect, but inescapable, fashion the departure of Winnie's mother accounts for the fact that, as we witnessed at the end of the last chapter, the Assistant Commissioner is poised to enter Verloc's shop in order to interview the prime suspect in the Greenwich affair. We will discover that Stevie was labelled with his address by Winnie to assuage the anxiety of mother and sister lest the simple-minded young man should get lost when he crossed London to visit the almshouse. That address tab found on the collar of the bomb victim's coat by Chief Inspector Heat, to provide a neatness of connection in the evidence that bemused both Heat and the Assistant Commissioner, leads, of course, directly to Verloc's shop. An action originally intended by Winnie's mother with an eye to Verloc's comfort and ease – as the necessary supports to secure Stevie's future – initiates a capricious train of events which will culminate in the finger of guilt pointing directly at Verloc.

It is the way in which Conrad structures the narrative that allows us to appreciate the blend of sombre, yet comic, elements implicit in ironies of the kind noted above. The time-sequence of the novel ensures that as an action is being described in the 'dramatic present', the reader is encouraged to look both to the past and to the future to judge its full implications. Because we know already much of what the future holds, we are placed in the privileged position of being able to see a pattern of events unfolding – our detachment is also enforced by the narrator's magisterial prose style – and enmeshing characters blindly in the consequences of actions which they are powerless to control (or even to comprehend). Many other ironies also hang from the decision of Winnie's mother to leave Brett Street. For instance, not only does Winnie, who shares exactly the same protective priorities as her mother, fail to appreciate the reasons for her mother's so carefully calculated scheme, it is also abundantly clear to the reader that Winnie's mother's self-sacrificing act was needless.

Until Winnie so persistently forced Stevie on Verloc's attention, the young man hardly came within the range of Verloc's attention. Any irksome responsibility Verloc may have felt about maintaining Stevie and providing a home for his mother certainly figured in a low position in the secret agent's current preoccupations. In fact, Verloc hardly notices that Winnie's mother has left Brett Street.

Characters' blindness, their mistaken assumptions and false premises, are, as is the case throughout the novel, a recurring source of irony. One thread running through Chapter 8 is Winnie's repeated failure to understand first her mother's actions, then Stevie's overexcited frame of mind during the journey to and from the alms house, and finally her husband's mood of complete desperation at the end of the day. Already we know, from what has become a kind of catchphrase repeated in many slightly different forms, that Winnie 'felt profoundly that things do not stand much looking into'. Winnie walks around in a perpetual cloud of unknowing; her obtuseness is a kind of defence mechanism against life. Almost as *leitmotivs* to this notion of singular obtuseness – the mistaken assumptions characters in the novel seem doomed to make – we might note in passing the way Winnie's mother manipulates the essentially incurious outlook of the gentlemen who administer the charitable trust of the victuallers' organisation, or even the 'hypothesis' which the cabby forms – and then to his credit dismisses – that in Stevie he has picked up 'a drunken young nipper'.

The chapter extends our insight into Stevie's character, and the incident involving Stevie's reaction to the horse and cabman makes clear why – once Winnie's persistence causes the connection to click in Verloc's mind – the young lad will seem to provide such an effective instrument for Verloc's purposes. While Stevie is so full of an easily aroused and deeply felt sympathy for the unjustly oppressed and so eager to exact retribution, he is, because of his maimed rationality, incapable of arriving at a solution. The fists simply clench impotently in his pockets. Conrad gives the reader no more than a hint (at the beginning of Chapter 11) of what Verloc had to do on those long walks we will soon see him sharing with Stevie in order to prime him for his task. Any extended treatment of their discussions would be superfluous. Given the respect for Verloc which has been engendered in Stevie by his sister, we can well imagine how easy it must have been for Verloc to exploit Stevie's susceptibilities and to arouse a tendency towards vicious reprisal. His righteous indignation simply needs to be pointed in a certain direction. Again, Conrad's wry irony underlines the way in which Winnie's iconoclastic remarks

to her brother about the police have already started what will be for
Verloc a straightforward business of indoctrination.

Chapter 9

Summary
Verloc returns from his trip to the continent. There is no change in
his despondent mood. Over breakfast Winnie declares that, although
Stevie has been missing his mother, he has been making himself very
useful. She sings the young man's praises and commends the loyalty
he feels towards Verloc. In the meantime, she has to intervene to
calm Stevie's outraged feelings of sympathy for the charwoman, Mrs
Neale, who exploits Stevie's compassion by telling him of the
harshness of her life; she then spends the small amounts of money
Stevie gives her on drink.

Verloc is surprised when his wife suggests that he should take
Stevie for a walk. She assures Verloc that her brother will not get
lost, but she does not disclose the reason for her certainty on this
point. These walks soon become almost a daily routine for the pair,
and Winnie congratulates herself on having brought her husband and
brother closer together.

The reader begins to be aware that a plan is forming in Verloc's
mind. His gloom is somewhat lightened, though Stevie's increasingly
frequent moods of violent frustration worry Winnie, who puts them
down to the influence of her husband's anarchist associates. At this
point we understand that Verloc, realising how useful Stevie might be
in furthering plans for the bomb outrage demanded by Vladimir, has
already begun his indoctrination. Apparently in response to Winnie's
anxiety about her brother, Verloc suggests that a change of air might
do Stevie some good. Why should Stevie not spend a few days with
Michaelis at his cottage in the countryside? Winnie agrees.

Winnie is now left to spend a good deal of time on her own. On the
day of the Greenwich explosion when Verloc returns home she finds
him huddled over the fire, his teeth chattering uncontrollably.
Winnie thinks her husband must have caught a cold. Verloc cannot
eat the supper she has prepared. He reveals he has withdrawn all
their savings from the bank, and he talks of emigrating, an idea that
Winnie rejects forthrightly, with her commitment to Stevie very
much to the fore of her mind. Having surprised herself by the
intensity of her rejection of her husband's proposal, she turns on him
the force of her sexual attraction, but just at this moment the shop
bell rings.

When Verloc returns from the shop he is white-faced with shock. The lean stranger who awaits Verloc is, of course, the Assistant Commissioner. Winnie asks her husband whether this man is one of the 'embassy people' about whom he has been talking in his sleep, a reference which prompts Verloc to a fiery outburst against such people and from which we gather his intention is to make a complete confession which will incriminate Vladimir. Before her husband leaves with the stranger, Winnie has the presence of mind to relieve Verloc of the money which he has withdrawn from the bank.

Shortly afterwards, Heat arrives in the shop in search of Verloc. To his disgust, Heat discovers from Winnie's description that his superior has lost no time in following the trail to Brett Street. Although Heat has insisted that his visit is in a purely private capacity, he tells Winnie of his official position and he cannot resist attempting to elicit information from her, particularly as Winnie's impassivity gives Heat the impression that she knows more than is really the case. He learns with some satisfaction that Winnie's brother is currently staying with Michaelis, since Heat had been originally hoping that Verloc would be able to provide him with information that would incriminate Michaelis; in the course of Heat's questioning he is led to tell Winnie, somewhat brutally, about the bomb explosion in Greenwich Park. Finally, Heat produces the piece of cloth which bears the Brett Street address. Winnie, still puzzled, acknowledges that the item is indeed from the collar of her brother's coat. By now Heat has realised that the second man involved in planning the explosion must have been Verloc.

When Verloc returns to the shop, he takes Heat into the parlour. Winnie, with uncharacteristic eagerness, eavesdrops on the conversation and, with mounting emotion, learns the terrible truth of Stevie's fate and her husband's responsibility for it. Heat, still waging his tactical battle against the Assistant Commissioner, warns Verloc not to place any faith in promises of official protection. Heat still feels deep resentment at what he sees as his superior's interference, and he recognises that a full confession from Verloc, followed by the attendant publicity, would destroy whole areas of secret information which he might have used at the appropriate time and disrupt a system of surveillance which he has carefully built up over the years. With these factors in mind, Heat suggests that Verloc would be best advised to make good his escape while he can. The Chief Inspector tells Verloc that the police will not pursue him and, because many of Verloc's associates believe that it was he who perished in the explosion, the disappearance of the secret agent might be effected easily.

The chapter closes with Heat giving only a cursory glance at Winnie as he leaves the shop, where Winnie remains alone and motionless, the glitter of her wedding ring surrounded by the trashy merchandise of her husband's ostensible business.

Commentary
This chapter simultaneously brings the police investigation to its climax and the Verloc marriage to a crisis. The perspective is largely that of Winnie: it is through her eyes that *we* recognise the formation and preparation of Verloc's plan. The realisation, unwittingly forced on Verloc by his wife, of Stevie's usefulness as a potential bomb carrier must have struck Verloc as being almost providential: it appeals to his temperamental disinclination to engage in the 'dirty work' himself or to expose himself unduly to risks. We also note from Winnie's point of view the dramatic changes in Stevie, the true cause of which she cannot appreciate: 'His expression was proud, apprehensive, and concentrated, like that of a small child entrusted for the first time with a box of matches and the permission to strike a light.' The reader recognises that Stevie is obviously being invited to engage in producing a firework display beyond that of his wildest dreams – and with a free conscience: his benefactor, the 'good' Mr Verloc desires it, and he will be striking a blow on behalf of all the decrepit cabhorses and Mrs Neales of this world.

Winnie's blissful ignorance, from which by the end of the chapter she will finally emerge, ensures that until her terrifying moment of truth the whole situation in which she finds herself is fraught with irony. There are clear dramatic ironies of the kind which derive from Winnie congratulating herself on inspiring in her husband a newly awakened paternal interest in Stevie; there are more minor, but telling, verbal ironies of the variety which issue from Winnie's assurance that Stevie 'would go through fire' for her husband, or from her instruction, before her brother goes to stay in the country with Michaelis, that Stevie should not dirty his clothes unduly. Some readers may find the accumulation of this sort of irony unnecessarily heartless, but it is important to understand that the narrator, though he clearly has a penchant for grim humour, does not wish the reader to savour these ironies purely for their own sake. Irony for Conrad is a tool for moral analysis and discrimination. Through it, he points up the end result of Winnie's constitutional obtuseness. Again, as was indicated in connection with the previous chapter, it is by means of irony that Conrad impresses on the reader an understanding of the way the whirligig of time operates. Characters in the novel are not in control of their fate; their actions invariably lead to 'purposes mistook'. The structure of the novel frequently makes us consider how easily events might have taken a different turn. This is the irony of 'if only . . .' For instance, how unfortunate it has proved to be from Verloc's point of view that Winnie characteristically did not tell her husband just why she was so certain Stevie would not get lost. The price that has to be paid for the Verlocs' habitual failure to communicate with one another is the vital piece of evidence from Stevie's collar. It costs Verloc dear. We note, too, that Heat arrives only a few moments after the Assistant Commissioner has left with Verloc. What if Heat had arrived *before* his superior? Time plays strange tricks in the novel. Remember, Heat is looking for Verloc's assistance in providing information which will allow him to incriminate Michaelis. The Chief Inspector might have been prepared to suppress all kinds of evidence, as long as it suited his own interest. In fact, Heat behaves in this chapter in a way which shamefully makes a nonsense of his distinction between the roles of a private citizen and a public official. Even at this stage of the game, his animus against the Assistant Commissioner who has outmanoeuvred him, and his desire to maintain his own network of power by salvaging as much as he can of the *status quo* which suited him, lead him to advise Verloc not to trust the Assistant Commissioner and to escape while the going is good. Moreover, how anomalous it is that it should be the normally secretive Heat who, while seeking to find out more information from Winnie in the absence of her husband, discloses information to her which he had no intention of revealing when he first entered the shop. Heat is ironically pushed in this direction by the feeling that Winnie's air of unflappability must mean she knows more than is really the case. In fact, Winnie in one sense does 'know' a lot; however, it is not until Heat blunders into telling her what took place in Greenwich Park that she begins to arrange what she knows into any explicatory pattern.

From a structural point of view, this chapter and its place in the plot of the novel will repay close study (see p.75).

Chapter 10

Summary
The Assistant Commissioner returns to Westminister to seek out the Secretary of State as he had promised. After Toodle's initial impression that the Assistant Commissioner has failed in his mission has been quickly corrected, the Assistant Commissioner is ushered into the presence of Sir Ethelred to whom he communicates what he has discovered from Verloc's freely volunteered confession. His account

involves a summary which clears Michaelis of any suspicion of guilt in the affair, outlines Vladimir's part in the plot and identifies Verloc's weak-minded brother-in-law as the unintended victim of the explosion, though the Assistant Commissioner has clearly been given no conception of the nature of Stevie's fanatical devotion to Verloc. The Assistant Commissioner, awaiting further instructions as to how he should proceed, assures Sir Ethelred that Verloc will not make any attempt to escape: he lacks the energy; moreover Verloc has emphasised that his wife is steadfastly opposed to any idea of flight abroad.

Having reflected on a parallel between the attitude of Verloc's wife and his own wife's objection to his working abroad, the Assistant Commissioner returns home, changes and then leaves for the salon of Michaelis's patroness; he informs the lady of her protégé's innocence of any connection with the Greenwich affair. Vladimir is also among the guests at the great lady's house and, on leaving, the Assistant Commissioner waits for the diplomat and takes some pleasure in revealing to him the successful outcome of his recent inquiries, which reflect considerable credit on the efficiency of the British police and which will provide the impetus needed to rid the country of political spies and *agents provocateurs* employed by embassies such as Vladimir's. The two men part outside the Assistant Commissioner's club, an establishment which the Assistant Commissioner does not think Vladimir is likely to frequent in the future. The Assistant Commissioner reflects on how quickly the time has passed during his full and productive evening.

Commentary
This chapter appears to conclude the police investigation. It is the last time we shall see not only the Assistant Commissioner, but also Sir Ethelred, Toodles, Michaelis's patroness and Vladimir. The chapter provides us also with a kind of buffer between the final image of Winnie in Chapter 9 and the part she will play in the sequel – the narrator makes us wait to see how Winnie will react to Stevie's death. Because we know more than the Assistant Commissioner, we suspect that his certainty that the case may now be neatly concluded is likely to be undermined. Assuredly, the nature of the political motivation behind the bomb outrage may have been revealed, but the reader will soon discover that, even as the Assistant Commissioner congratulates himself on an expedient conclusion to the case and complacently assumes that Verloc safely awaits any decision as to what action will be taken against him, the secret agent is meeting a very different fate at Winnie's hands. For, as the Assistant Commissioner glimpses

briefly, there is a 'domestic' dimension to the drama; however, his ignorance of Winnie's passionate attachment to Stevie means he can have no conception that, metaphorically, there is another bomb ticking away – this time in Brett Street. He comments wryly that when he met Verloc he found himself in the presence of a bizarre 'psychological state', but his knowledge of its full implications is necessarily limited – just as limited as his perspective, based on the assumptions of a man who moves easily through the corridors of power of the English establishment, on Verloc's reaction to Vladimir's plot, which seems to the Assistant Commissioner to be incomprehensible, almost a 'ferocious joke'. In the widest terms of the novel, the Assistant Commissioner's pride in his own perception and his management of a case which is now virtually 'sewn up', invites *nemesis*. In *The Secret Agent*, Conrad delights in showing the reader the ways in which experience has an inexorable way of exploding all the characters' assumptions about the nature of reality – even those of the most active and intelligent character in the whole novel. The sudden death of the crucial witness and the flight, quickly followed by the 'inexplicable' suicide, of his murderer, will leave what the newspaper report will later describe as 'an impenetrable mystery' hanging over the whole Greenwich affair. In this light, the shared sense of certainty in the conversation in Sir Ethelred's room will finally take on a very shadowy quality.

It is entirely appropriate that after reporting his success to Sir Ethelred, the Assistant Commissioner should visit the house of the patroness of Michaelis: 'he knew he would be welcome there'. The reassurance he is able to give the great lady of Michaelis's innocence might almost be uttered with a mental note of 'mission accomplished', for it is the nature of his private connection with the lady – or more particularly his troublesome wife's connection with her – which has in one sense predetermined his whole approach to the case. The glimpse we get of the Explorers' Club in the final paragraph of the chapter also implicitly suggests the strong undercurrent of personal concern that has run through the Assistant Commissioner's management of the Greenwich affair. He imagines that Vladimir will be excluded from the Club; but more important, perhaps, is the underlying suggestion that now the Assistant Commissioner's wife's connection with the great lady is no longer under threat, his own formula of peace – the daily whist party at the Club which offers a 'drug against the secret ills of existence' (see Chapter 5) – is secured for the future. His wife has rendered real 'exploration' unattainable; this man of energy will settle for his retreat.

Vladimir is also present at the house of the great lady, and we are given a final and illuminating new perspective on him. At first we see him offering an urbane version of his scaremongering stories to some of the guests, a reminder of his more brutally manipulative approach to Verloc in Chapter 2. But the intimidator of the secret agent is quickly put on the defensive in another of those two-handed dialogues that thread the novel. Confronted with the Assistant Commissioner and a startlingly rapid discovery of his guilt, it is now Vladimir's turn to feel threatened and anxious about his own position. Conrad emphasises the extent to which Vladimir's habits of mind are the inevitable product of generations of conditioning in an autocratic nation.

Chapter 11

Summary
The narrative returns to the Verloc *ménage*, where the action was left suspended at the end of Chapter 9. Verloc, gratified that at least Heat has relieved him of the responsibility of having to break the news of Stevie's death to his wife, reflects on the unforeseen consequences which have led to the failure of his plans: Stevie's clumsiness in Greenwich and Winnie's sewing of the address label in the boy's coat without telling him. However, he determines to suppress his annoyance with his wife on this latter point. He appreciates that Winnie is temporarily gripped by the immediate shock of bereavement; he is sympathetic in his feelings, though it is clear that he has no conception of the depth of his wife's attachment to Stevie. Verloc feels that he needs to calm Winnie's grief so that they may sensibly discuss plans for the future, for he expects the police to take him away the next day. But when he assures Winnie that he meant her brother no harm, she does not reply. She remains motionless, locked in her grief. Emotionally drained and in a fatalistic mood, Verloc nevertheless finds he is hungry and he withdraws to the parlour where he carves for himself some of the cold beef that Winnie had previously left out for him. When Verloc returns to Winnie and tries physically to arouse her from her immobility, she wrestles herself from him and runs from the shop into the kitchen.

Somewhat exasperated by his wife's behaviour, Verloc reflects on how close his plans had come to a complete success, which would have increased his prestige as a secret agent. Again, he tries to break through the habitual state of uncommunicativeness between Winnie and himself by confiding in her that she can have no idea of the pressure that was applied to him by that 'brute' Vladimir, a recollection which provokes in Verloc a spurt of professional pride in his former services as a secret agent – both to his embassy employers and to the cause of social stability – and a feeling of outrage that these services should have been set at nought. The fury of his indignation and the novelty of taking his wife into his confidence about his secret life make Verloc forget for a moment the reality of Stevie's fate, though finally, doing his best to be understanding, he recommends 'a good cry' to Winnie as the best way of relieving her grief.

The narrator now shifts the perspective and takes us inside Winnie's mind. Sitting hunched in Stevie's old place in the kitchen, Winnie feels an increasing revulsion towards her husband; her numbed mind is dominated by a sense of betrayal; she remembers that from her earliest days her whole life has been centred on her protective love for Stevie; she recalls the need to defend Stevie from a violent father, which first fostered the fiercest kind of maternal feelings towards her brother, and the rejection of romance in her youth in order to secure Stevie's future by marriage to Verloc.

Oblivious to his wife's feelings, Verloc continues to vow vengeance against his embassy employers: his full confession will expose all their dealings to the public. While he rants on, or later more calmly returns to his plans for Winnie to keep the shop going during his period of imprisonment, nearly all his words wash over Winnie, who is totally preoccupied with the idea that her husband is the man who took away and destroyed the one person she cherished. And it was her blindness that prevented her seeing what was happening. When Verloc enlarges on his plans to escape retribution from his revolutionary associates on his release from prison, Winnie hears the words only as an assertion of a wish to gain impunity by escaping abroad. Suddenly it dawns on Winnie that now Stevie is dead, she has been released from all ties to Verloc. She is a free woman. She goes upstairs, and during her absence Verloc partakes ravenously of some more cold beef.

When his wife re-appears, she is dressed to go out, and Verloc assumes that she intends to fly off to her mother. Nothing could be further from Winnie's thoughts. In fact, she is uncertain about what use to make of her new freedom, but her latest intention had been simply to leave the house for ever. Now she sits down, and Verloc lectures her on her wifely responsibilities: her place is with him this evening. Winnie, however, misinterprets Verloc's words that 'I can't let you go out, old girl', which take on for her a sinister overtone. How can she escape? Her mind turns to the idea of physical resistance, for which she will need a weapon. Meanwhile, with some exasperation, Verloc defends his actions once again; Stevie's death was a pure accident; he reminds Winnie that because she pushed the boy so eagerly in his direction at a time of crisis, she is just as much responsible for Stevie's death as he is.

Wearily, Verloc flings himself on the sofa. When he growls that he wishes he had never seen Greenwich Park, this triggers in Winnie's mind a vivid image of her brother's dismemberment as a result of the explosion. But at this very moment Verloc believes that the time is ripe for reconciliation; he is sure that Winnie must have seen by now the force of his arguments; moreover, he believes that his wife loves him for himself. So Verloc calls Winnie over to him in the tone which usually signals the prelude to the couple's love-making. Yet when Winnie does come, it is not for reconciliation. Certain that she has been released from every marital obligation, she savagely plunges a carving knife into Verloc's breast, a blow which at the last, drawn-out instant Verloc perceives, but is powerless to avoid. After a few moments, Winnie's euphoria – her sense of complete liberation after striking the blow – passes and, realising what she has done, she rushes from the room. From the door she notices Verloc's hat rocking slightly in the middle of the floor.

Commentary

As the narrator passes back and forth from Verloc's perspective to that of Winnie, it is like the issuing of reports on two minds separated by a no-man's-land of virtually total misunderstanding. Neither partner can understand the other, because to do so they would have to cease to be themselves. The whole marriage, of course, has always been marked by a congenital absence of communication. In the past non-communication seemed on both sides to oil the works of their peculiar marital arrangement and to satisfy each partner's different requirements. Conrad's ironic treatment of the relationship reaches its acme in Chapter 11 and emphasises in severe moral terms, which are nevertheless shot through with a farcical appreciation of the situation, the price that must be paid for emotional obtuseness and intellectual blindness which, on both sides, have ensured that the real self of each partner remains a misconceived fiction.

While Winnie is benumbed by the blackest oppression of spirit she has ever known, for Verloc, in one sense, the dark night of his little soul is over. Certainly *he* feels the worst is past. True, he has partially discovered the Conradian nightmare that to act is to commit oneself to an uncharted sea; but the fact that all his carefully laid plans have been deflected from their purpose by the irresistible workings of circumstance is not something that Verloc feels with any great, tragic intensity; he finds a refuge in a facile kind of fatalistic resignation. He now wishes to look to the future: 'making the best of things' is the appropriate cliché for him. In fact, his temperamental failure to begin to appreciate the full enormity of what, from Winnie's point of view, he has done, is summed up in the string of clichés that pass his lips: he advises his wife that what is done is done; there is no point in crying over spilt milk; she needs to pull herself together; perhaps a good cry would do her good; and so on. To Verloc, Stevie's death is regrettable, but it is essentially something which he sees as one of life's reverses; it can finally be glossed over. His fundamental error is, of course, his failure to recognise that Stevie is his wife's *raison d'être*; certainly, Stevie is *the* reason why Winnie married him, yet Verloc believes he is loved for himself. This fatal misunderstanding makes Verloc's self-absorption assume ludicrous proportions in this scene, for though we should not ignore that within his limited compass he is sympathetically concerned with his wife's grief, most of what he has to say to her continually comes back to himself – his justifications, his forbearance, his wounded pride, his plans for the future, the intolerable pressure he was under, and so on. But Winnie does not care for *him* at all.

Conrad's irony plays around the way in which at virtually every point of their 'discussion – it is, in fact, a monologue of which isolated parts impinge upon Winnie's consciousness – Verloc unwittingly acts and speaks in a way which undermines his whole intention of assisting Winnie to ride out quickly what he sees as the passing squall of her bereavement. Every word she hears deepens her revulsion towards him; every move tips the balance closer to his own murder. The shortest list of Verloc's counter-productive insensitivities might include the declaration of his impunity from the revolutionist's knife, the manner in which he reminds Winnie of her responsibility in forcing Stevie in his attention at a time of crisis, and his mention of Greenwich Park, which so palpably brings to his wife's imagination an image of Stevie's dismembered body. This series of miscalculated moves culminates in the awesome misunderstanding of the call to love-making which is the prelude to Verloc's death. While Verloc is anticipating the pleasures of some reconciliatory sexual intercourse, his wife comes with murderous intention.

We may recall that earlier in Verloc's life an entanglement with a woman, a *femme fatale*, had led to unfortunate consequences, a fact which Vladimir humiliatingly elicited from him. No doubt, from Verloc's point of view – remember his profession is in part that of a vendor of pornography – Winnie had always seemed to satisfy with apparently guaranteed security the slimy lust she had first provoked in him as his eyes focused on her from above the bed clothes in Winnie's mother's lodging-house. In one sense, Verloc has used her over seven years of marriage just as destructively as he exploited Stevie. At bottom the motives of an indolent self-gratification and self-protection spring from the same egotism. In the following chapter Winnie will, for Ossipon's benefit, briefly allude to the repugnance she has felt in Verloc's embraces: 'he loved me till I sometimes wished myself—' (she draws back from the word 'dead'). This locates the part of the iceberg of their relationship that is generally hidden beneath the surface; however, Conrad's implicit treatment of the Verloc's sexual relationship is an object lesson to many later novelists who believe that only a full action replay version of sexual encounters may lay bare the secrets of the libido. In this climactic scene, when her husband calls Winnie to act out her usual passive sexual acceptance, we may well appreciate the added force his note of wooing gives to the fatal blow. She sees only through a blur of passion which demands retribution, but the reader recognises that as she moves across to the sofa she brings to Verloc a bizarre variation of his 'little death'; she will penetrate him – with a carving knife.

If Verloc is obtuse, Winnie's responses throughout the chapter match his at every false step. When she does register what Verloc says, it is only to attribute to them a monstrous meaning which, in an understandable way, is the creation of her obsessed state of mind. And when Winnie is driven into action, believing that Verloc is threatening her very life, what a contrast this makes with the stolidity her character has generally suggested. At first, her newly discovered freedom seems to have nowhere to go. Yet as she moves murderously across the parlour to kill Verloc, she achieves the kind of hard clarity of destructive impulse, a liberation from all moral and social conventions, that a Karl Yundt would admire. It is not, however, a justifying political ideology that motivates Winnie; it is rather an instinctive, atavistic urge: 'into that plunging blow, delivered over the side of the couch, Mrs Verloc had put all the inheritance of her immemorial and obscure descent, the simple ferocity of the age of caverns, and the unbalanced nervous fury of the age of bar-rooms'. She is the animal whose cub has been snatched from it. She acts as Stevie's avenger. Indeed, the narrator draws our attention to the fact that she even looks like Stevie as she moves to plunge the knife into Verloc – 'as if the homeless soul of Stevie had flown for shelter to the breast of his sister'. Is Conrad suggesting that the spring of the truest form of anarchism lies in this primitive, bestial, degenerative aspect of human experience? All the talk about anarchism that has gone on in Verloc's parlour has been so much hot air. In one sense, leaving to one side the Professor's preparedness to destroy himself, Winnie and Stevie are the true anarchists of the novel: they commit the only genuine anarchist acts; both are self-destructive.

At certain moments, Conrad brings home to us the horror of the events he describes. Verloc's voracious swallowing of the cold beef – 'laid out in the likeness of funeral baked meats for Stevie's obsequies' – enacts in a symbolic way the nature of his preying on Stevie and, linking with other images in the novel of torn or cannibalised flesh, it emphasises Verloc's monstrous culpability which might be partially obscured by his own complacent evasions. The description of Verloc's death also enforces on the reader a peculiar form of horror because Verloc is given time 'to taste the flavour of death'. The account of that final, drawn-out moment before the knife descends into his breast, which in terms of measured time is a mere split second, is a *tour de force* of Conrad's use of perspective; in miniature, it also mimics the novel's whole technique of a slow, meticulous unfolding of events. For we are made to appreciate Verloc's final terror in a grim slow-motion and from the point of view of the murdered man himself. However, though there are moments of horror – and pathos, too – which involve a certain identification with the plights of Verloc and Winnie, the narrator's controlling perspective of aloof detachment and scorn dictates what he judges to be the appropriate emotional register. Style and presentation manipulate the reader's response. We are not invited to wallow in a steamy bath of melodramatic emotion; neither are we encouraged to grant these two characters a tragic status.

The tone is mock-heroic; the setting is emphatically *petit bourgeois*; the action is more akin to farce than tragedy. Notice the nature of the stage, for instance: the setting is first Verloc's squalid shop and then the familiar domestic interior of kitchen and parlour. Think also of the details of the scene that remain in the mind: they include a carving knife – the use of this prop has been most carefully prepared – a sofa, Verloc's hat and blood which, ticking like a clock, falls on the floorcloth. The narrator, in a sardonic way, savours the mundane, vulgar trappings of the domestic drama. And what about the characters' speech? As we have already observed, Verloc expresses himself volubly in a string of clichés; our heroine is almost completely taciturn. When we are taken inside their minds, the technique of the narrated interior monologue passes their thoughts and feelings through the filter of the narrator's scorn and formal precision of language, thus producing an incongruous effect that points up the essentially threadbare quality of thought and feeling which is described: 'His [Verloc's] intention was not to overwhelm his wife with bitter reproaches. Mr Verloc felt no bitterness. The unexpected march of events had converted him to the doctrine of fatalism.' This chapter is also notable for the relatively large number of direct interventions the narrator himself makes to point up an irony or to emphasise a moral observation. Moreover, the narrator constantly constantly draws our attention to the macabre element of farce that runs through the whole scene. Much of it, of course, is produced by the ironies of misconstruction and cross-purposes which attain an almost ludicrous exaggeration, but we are also invited to observe such details as the amusing appropriateness of the way in which the constitutionally indolent secret agent takes his death lying down and 'without stirring a limb'. The narrator seems to view events, even at the moment of their greatest climax, from the heights of a magisterial aloofness – or even a poised contemptuousness.

Chapter 12

Summary

Driven into a frenzy by her hysterical fear of hanging, Winnie staggers out into the dark street. She feels totally isolated; she dismisses the idea of going to her mother and drags herself along, thinking confusedly of suicide and then of the remote possibility of escape abroad. At this moment she is found by Ossipon who, having left the Silenus (see the end of Chapter 4), has been walking the streets alone for two hours before plucking up courage to visit the shop in Brett street and press his parasitic attentions on Verloc's widow. Ossipon is greatly surprised when his would-be prey throws herself into his arms and immediately assumes a relationship of close intimacy. In her crisis, Winnie's formerly suppressed attraction to Ossipon is openly revealed: her feelings suggest that the robust anarchist is to be her 'saviour'. Ossipon hardly needs to go through the motions of declaring his love to win her to his side.

The couple are, of course, totally at cross-purposes in their view of the present situation. Ossipon believes that Verloc perished in the explosion at Greenwich Park; Winnie, in her confused state, imagines that Ossipon, almost by some kind of sympathetic intuition, has realised that she has been forced to kill her devil of a husband. Ossipon, struck by Winnie's passionate frenzy and the revelation of her bitter hatred for Verloc, considers the possibility that Verloc may have been driven to suicide to escape this woman; his fear and suspicion are further aroused when Winnie tells him of the visits by the police to Brett Street and when she lets drop Verloc's connection with an embassy. Ossipon has the most threatening sense of entering deep waters, but he appears to go along with Winnie's idea that they should flee the country together. He learns from Winnie that she has on her person all the money from her husband's bank account.

Ossipon remembers that there is a boat-train they can catch from Waterloo which will take them to the continent, but before they leave for the station Winnie recalls that she has left the shop open. When they return to the shop, she is anxious that Ossipon should turn off the light in the parlour, towards which she pushes him. Ossipon enters; in swift juxtaposition, he receives two hammer-blow shocks. There on the sofa, apparently sleeping, is Verloc, the man Ossipon thought had been blown to pieces in Greenwich Park. Ossipon's mind reels. Have the Verlocs laid some kind of trap for him? Then he sees the knife in Verloc's breast, and with a sickening intensity the truth dawns on him.

Ossipon is terrified by the implications of the whole situation – both those foreseen and those unforeseeable – into which he has been drawn; he is terrified most particularly by the clinging attentions of the woman he now knows to be a murderess. However, as he feels there is at present no other course of action open to him, he takes a cab with Winnie to Waterloo. During the journey he relieves Winnie of her money, having established that it probably cannot be traced back to Verloc, and instructs her how they must behave at the station before the train leaves in order to avoid drawing any attention to the fact that they are travelling together. After several brandies in the station bar to fortify himself, Ossipon joins Winnie in the compartment just before the train is due to leave. While Winnie lovingly regards Ossipon as her 'saviour', Ossipon has been increasingly struck by a resemblance between Winnie and her brother which he categorises as the type of a murderous degenerate. As the train is pulling away from the end of the platform, Ossipon leaps from the carriage and leaves Winnie to her fate. He spends the night aimlessly walking the gloomy London streets before returning home. Only when daylight comes does he sleep.

Commentary
The narrator has, of course, prepared for Ossipon's arrival at Brett Street, though again time plays strange tricks. What if Ossipon had arrived at the shop some time earlier, instead of prowling the streets indecisively for two hours? It is just possible that he might have prevented the build-up to a murder. There is a terrible irony, too, in the new turn events will take for Winnie: no sooner has she achieved her freedom by a perfect 'anarchist' act than she surrenders it to another man that 'fate' sends her. Whether she follows a self-

sacrificing calculation, or is driven by a vacuum of hopelessness and the need to be loved, both of the men she turns to as 'saviours' prove to be destroyers. The burnt fool's bandaged finger goes wobbling back to the fire. It is Winnie's congenital obtuseness that, in both cases, is largely responsible for the catastrophe. Her central involvement in this scene will ensure that it is just as full of an absurd sense of cross-purposes as the last one. Ossipon sees Winnie initially as a potential romantic conquest – and as a source of funds. Winnie, who has long noticed his glances of what she interprets as 'love', attributes a depth to them of which Ossipon is constitutionally incapable. She sees him as 'a radiant messenger of life'. Their very different needs and motives seem to draw them together. For a time each sees what he or she wants to see in the other: for instance, Ossipon's vanity at first accounts for Winnie's eager response to him, though very soon he will be looking for the exit to this relationship. The end product is, for Winnie, suicide; for Ossipon, it is an inescapable guilt which shatters his vulturine existence.

The turning-point of the scene occurs when Winnie, so anxious to have the light in the parlour switched off, pushes Ossipon into the room. In the context of the Verlocs' bedroom, the turning off of the light symbolised the couple's habitual uncommunicativeness which locked each partner within his or her own perception of reality. At this point in the narrative, with a nice variation on the symbolism, Winnie's direction, 'Go in and put it out – or I'll go mad', forces Ossipon to experience a revelation of blinding, almost deranging intensity. Such will be his horror at what is revealed that, when darkness does finally fall on Verloc's corpse, it is only because – again at Winnie's insistence – the electricity is fumblingly cut off at the meter in the shop. On no account will Ossipon return to the parlour.

At the moment when Ossipon experiences those two revelatory blows which rock him to the innermost core of his being, we see with what consummate craftsmanship Conrad has prepared for the effect. At this point all the weight of Conrad's skills of narrative construction comes to rest. The shifting of time-schemes and perspective and the manipulation of the different locations of the novel's action have, moreover, created a climax which encapsulates one of *The Secret Agent's* recurring preoccupations. It concerns the way in which the view of 'reality' that characters create in their own minds is so often a distorted one – because of the pressures of their routine existences, their prejudices, self-interests, lack of imagination, or their being forced into simplifying constructions of the way things are which result from a lack of access to the complexity of knowledge that only the omniscient narrator of this novel can achieve. Ossipon's assumption that Verloc met his death in Greenwich Park is understandable enough, given what he learnt from the Professor in the Silenus. But in an instant that assumption crashes headlong into the palpable reality of Mr Verloc who is apparently in a characteristic posture on the sofa. Then in the 'long moment' of stunned and sickened response, Ossipon receives the second blow: the knife indicates to him that his original assumption was, ironically, partially correct; Verloc *is* dead, but he has met his death in a fashion that Ossipon could hardly have begun to imagine. (The prose style of this passage is examined in some depth later; see p.80.)

The final climax of the chapter also follows an inexorable design. Given the precise nature of the situation – and of Ossipon – his desertion of Winnie will follow from the discovery of her husband's corpse as one more link in the causal chain. The combinations of occurrences in a time-sequence appear to fall haphazardly, but as we near the end of the novel we sense the completion of a pattern: the contingencies of experience slam shut like the door of a prison.

Chapter 13

Summary

Ossipon and the Professor are found in the latter's shabby room, which is the centre of his bomb-making activities. The Professor mentions that he has visited Michaelis, who is still hard at work on his autobiography and knows nothing of Verloc's death. The Professor's scorn for Michaelis's mild, utopian views prompts him to define his own scenario for a future which will belong to a master race who have the strength to exterminate the weak.

The two men take an omnibus to the Silenus. The sight of the crowds thronging the streets oppresses the Professor. He asks Ossipon why he seems to have been plunged into gloom recently. By the time they reach the Silenus, Ossipon has still not disclosed any reason for his depression, but he is obviously haunted by some phrases from a newspaper cutting which is ten days old; the cutting gives an account of the mysterious disappearance of a woman from a Cross-Channel boat before it arrived at France.

When the Professor remarks that the 'little legacy', which it is said Ossipon has come into, has not had much effect on his spirits, Ossipon offers the money to the Professor; the Professor simply promises to send him a bill for some chemicals he needs. The two men leave the Silenus, Ossipon to continue what seems an inevitable descent into dissolution; the Professor, to walk through the crowds he despises, 'like a pest in the street full of men'.

Commentary
The final scene of the novel takes us back to the same location and two characters we met in Chapter 4. This reminds us of when we first heard a report of the bomb in Greenwich Park and of the complexity of motivation that has been revealed to us since the initial assumption that it was Verloc who perished in the explosion. In Chapter 13 it is now the Professor's turn confidently to state another hypothesis: the police have managed to smooth over the Greenwich affair by murdering Verloc. Ossipon does not bother to enlighten the Professor. In fact, we are to assume that, because of Verloc's death, it will be impossible for the authorities to attach any specific guilt to those at the embassy who had instigated the explosion. The whole affair, from every point of view except that of the misguided Professor, is far from being neatly smoothed over. No single person in the novel knows precisely what has happened, or why, though Ossipon's knowledge of the last act of the drama has left him a broken man. One of the last twists in the case is that the Professor will be the unwitting beneficiary of Verloc's money. The earnings gained by the secret agent as an embassy spy and a self-proclaimed defender of the stability of society, will now go to finance the Professor's bombs; it is a fact which forges a final ironic connection between the Verlocs' domestic drama and its impact on the wider public sphere, and underlines in a characteristically Conradian way the self-cancelling nature of most human action.

On the last occasion the narrative was located in the Silenus, we heard of what proved to be Stevie's death from a newspaper account. The final perspective we have of his sister's death is a newspaper cutting which is obviously well-creased as a result of Ossipon's obsession with it. On the face of it, the report is a mere hackneyed piece of journalism and we will be struck by its inadequacy: we have been placed in the position of knowing so much more than this limited perspective which can only finally register a sense of 'impenetrable mystery'. In fact, this fragmentary, rather oblique treatment of Winnie's death produces a powerful pathos. (This point is discussed at further length on p.67.)

In his 'Author's Note', Conrad wrote of following 'Winnie Verloc's story to its anarchistic end of utter desolation and despair'. Those are, indeed, the predominant final notes. Ossipon walks towards the gutter of what seems his inevitable personal fragmentation; only the

Professor possesses any sense of purpose as he moves through the London streets with his neo-fascist mentality and his mission of random destruction. Nevertheless, the epithet that is finally applied to him is that of a 'pest', which suggests that though he may make for himself (and others) a small hole into eternity, it will essentially produce only the effect of a minor nuisance in the largely indifferent scheme of things. The action of the novel has suggested that all attempts to influence 'the street full of men' are doomed to appear futile. The stolid weight of numbers of the crowds and the inevitable passing of time in an endless series of moments will ensure that the Professor's mark leaves only the smallest of scratches on the surface of existence. Perhaps it is Conrad's view, as expressed in the novel, that in the final reckoning even the extremes of self-sacrificing love or vicious hatred are equally ineffectual. Yet in adopting this position at the end of *The Secret Agent* we may pull ourselves up short with the realisation of the extent to which prolonged exposure has already infected us with the idea that the narrator's Olympian role in the novel is one that might be available to us as we face the nature of our quotidian reality.

4 THEMES AND ISSUES

4.1 FACING THE DARKNESS

One of Conrad's clearest statements of the view he holds of the world, the outlook that underpins his social and political thinking, occurs in a letter of 1897 to Cunninghame Graham. Graham, a friend of Conrad, held radical, socialist opinions very different from Conrad's. In response to Graham's belief in the idea of progress, Conrad wrote: 'you are a most hopeless idealist, – your aspirations are irrealisable.' He continued:

> There is a, let us say, a machine. It evolved itself (I am severely scientific) out of a chaos of scraps of iron and behold! – it knits. I am horrified at the horrible work and stand appalled. I feel it ought to embroider, – but it goes on knitting. You come and say: 'This is all right: It's only a question of the right kind of oil. Let us use this, – for instance, – celestial oil and the machine will embroider a most beautiful design in purple and gold.' Will it? Alas, no! You cannot by any special lubrication make embroidery with a knitting machine. And the most withering thought is that the infamous thing has made itself: made itself without thought, without conscience, without foresight, without eyes, without heart. It is a tragic accident, – and it has happened. You can't interfere with it. The last drop of bitterness is in the suspicion that you can't even smash it.

The universe of Conrad's novels is a void. Man attempts to avert his eyes from the void, but it is there all the same, waiting to engulf him. Some men may be protected from it by lack of imagination; some by finding in hard work or dedication to a cause the illusion of a purpose in the indifferent scheme of things; some by following the dictates of a simple moral code based essentially on an idea of fidelity. Yet the central episodes of Conrad's narratives invariably manoeuvre the protagonist into a position in which he is isolated from the reassuring supports and conventions of society and, by being thrown back on his last resources, forced to confront his own vulnerability and corruptibility. What is involved is the profoundest challenge to a character's identity – and to values, formerly taken for granted, which in extremity are revealed to be illusory or insubstantial. As test cases of this enforced facing up to an inner and outer darkness, readers who have a wider knowledge of Conrad's work have only to recall the effect on Marlow in *Heart of Darkness* (1902) of his journey in search of Kurtz, which takes him through the brooding, primeval African landscape to the upper reaches of the Congo, or the fate of Decoud in *Nostromo* (1904).

Decoud, a man of considerable sceptical intelligence, had been drawn by his love of a woman into the tangled web of politics and revolution in an inveterately unstable South American state. When at a moment of crisis he was isolated on a small island in the Placid Gulf, he 'found himself entertaining a doubt of his own individuality'; he was 'not fit to grapple with himself single-handed'; 'he beheld the universe as a succession of incomprehensible images. . . And all exertion seemed senseless.' After his suicide, as his body slipped into the untroubled waters of the Placid Gulf, Conrad comments that Decoud left not the slightest trace on 'the immense indifference of things', and, summing up one of the central facts of the Conradian universe, he adds: 'In our activity alone do we find the sustaining illusion of an independent existence as against the whole scheme of things of which we form a helpless part.'

Much more might be written on this topic, and a consideration, for instance, of the way in which a confrontation with the darkness affects the lives of Jim in *Lord Jim* (1900), or Razumov in *Under Western Eyes* (1911) or Heyst in *Victory* (1915) would be instructive. However, we need to concentrate at this stage on the way in which Conrad's sombre perception of the nature of the human condition is apparent in *The Secret Agent*.

Verloc's interview with Vladimir in Chapter 2, which is the motive force of the whole novel, might almost be seen as a burlesque version of those stressful and reductive confrontations, found so widely in Conrad's fiction, which expose the protagonist to precisely the peculiar combination of circumstances most calculated to subvert him. The keynote of *The Secret Agent* is mock-heroic, for it will immediately be apparent that the celebrated agent of the late Baron Stott-Wartenheim, 'so secret that he was never designated otherwise but by the symbol △', is not made of the stuff which will produce the struggle of a great soul against fate. Indeed, later in the novel, the Assistant Commissioner will wryly suggest to Sir Ethelred that Vladimir's call to action, and Verloc's response, might appear to be a 'ferocious joke'. However, it *is* a serious matter to Verloc because of his constitutional need to maintain an agreeably undemanding 'vocation' which sustains the security of his domestic ease. Moreover, Verloc has a certain professional pride; the secret nature of his work which allows him to pose – at least for his own eyes – as a protector of society, confers on him a reassuring status. The self-image is absurdly fraudulent, but the possibility, after the challenge of 'No work, no pay', of seeing his former existence slip away, produces a shudder to the deepest level of Verloc's soft bedrock of identity.

To reduce a mediocrity like Verloc to a state of black despair, no voyage down the Congo, no overwhelming moral dilemma, no extreme isolating circumstances are required. Yet, while Conrad's ironic treatment of the depression that descends on Verloc will encourage the reader to view the secret agent's response with an amused, if critical, detachment, for Verloc himself the enveloping nightmare is real enough. His whole life seems about to be ruined; he cannot sleep. The tenuous nature of his hold on existence is marvellously represented in Chapter 3, for instance, when as he undresses, Verloc is described as feeling that the fragile window-pane is all that separates his once apparently secure domestic retreat from a bleak, hostile world which is imaged in 'the enormity of cold, black, wet, muddy, inhospitable accumulation of bricks, slates and stones'. Throughout the novel Conrad repeatedly emphasises the cold indifference, or sometimes even the apparently inimical quality, which the objects of 'inorganic nature' seem to take on from a human perspective. Think, for example, of the mockingly cracked ring of the bell in Verloc's shop which portentously heralds so many little human dramas, or the incongruous and unpredictable janglings of the automatic piano in the Silenus. The cold wind of a world in which things do not care for man beats against Verloc's weak defences.

The dark night of Verloc's little soul seems to lift when Stevie is virtually offered to him in his hour of need. It is entirely characteristic of Verloc to feel that the way out of the darkness lies in getting somebody else to act on his behalf. The consequences of using a mentally retarded young man to plant a bomb are horrible, though Verloc will not feel his culpability in any extreme way; Stevie's death is to be regretted, but Verloc seems to imagine that the young man was in some way expendable. Even so, Verloc is hardly the diabolic monster he will inevitably – but, as far as he is concerned, unknowingly – appear to be in Winnie's eyes. T. S. Eliot once suggested, in connection with Baudelaire, that to have the capacity for damnation it is necessary to possess a great soul: 'the worst that can be said of most of our malefactors, from statesmen to thieves, is that they are not men enough to be damned'. Verloc may certainly be numbered among the hollow men; his sin is that of a morally inert spirit which sought the easy way out.

In this tendency, Verloc's behaviour – though it has particularly dramatic and inhuman consequences – is essentially all of a piece with the morality of nearly all the men and women in the novel. With the possible exception of the Professor, none of the characters we meet has the vigour to commit him- or herself to the darkness – or to the light. Leaving to one side for a moment the attempts at self-sacrifice by Winnie and her mother, the prevalent moral atmosphere of the novel may be summed up in the hackneyed formula of 'following the line of least resistance'. *The Secret Agent* presents us with lukewarm souls; they exist in a limbo of purposelessness which is proclaimed by the drab, damp streets of the metropolis through which they crawl. The Assistant Commissioner, one of the few lean and active characters who is not weighed down with flesh, may to a limited extent escape this censure, though behind his animation, so unusual in the world of this novel, there is the simple desire to preserve the sanctuary of whist games at his Club; and like virtually everyone else he twitches automatically, when called upon to act, to the impulses of self-interest.

A condign despair may come to even the moral cipher, however. The causal chain of events, forged initially by Vladimir, will fetter two other victims of the darkness. Winnie's insistence that things do not bear looking into, far from protecting her from the uncongenial, leads directly to her losing the one object of her love. After she learns how Stevie met his fate, she will find herself *in extremis*, and there is a genuine pathos at the end of the novel as we imagine the state of madness and despair which led to her suicide. Conrad's attitude to a moral nonentity like Ossipon, however, is one of unremitting scorn – even when he is defenceless. A traumatic guilt undermines such fraudulent evasions as the scientism of Lombroso, and at the end of the novel we see Ossipon's whole personality on the edge of collapse.

4.2 MISTAKEN PERSPECTIVES

Jocelyn Baines, in his fine biographical study of Conrad, is somewhat critical of *The Secret Agent*: 'The book lacks, unlike most of Conrad's work, a unifying theme, and when it is carefully examined falls apart into a succession of only superficially related scenes; in fact, the "crystallisation" of which Conrad speaks in the Author's Note never occurs.'

On one level it might appear that the novel possesses an unwieldy diversity, as we move from Verloc's shop in Soho to a foreign embassy, or from the Silenus beer-cellar to the inner sanctum of a Minister of State, and then off through the drab London streets to an almshouse. There are the elements of a detective investigation but, of themselves, they will hardly produce the 'crystallisation' Baines misses in the novel. In fact, that is not where Conrad's main interest lies.

In the first place, the novel is unified by the causal chain which is finally revealed to run through the widely spaced locales; the characters in *The Secret Agent* may appear to exist in discrete compartments, but their lives are shown to impinge on each other, though frequently in ways they cannot appreciate. Second, the atmosphere and moral climate of the novel are all-pervasive; torpor and drabness are the keynotes sounded by nearly every piece of description in the novel. The characters in their apparently separate spheres are nearly all infected by the same self-serving 'line of least resistance' morality. Third, all the characters are bound together, to a greater or lesser extent, by a condition of perennial mental blindness. The idea of the way in which characters perceive – or only partially perceive – reality runs through *The Secret Agent* and, supported by the novel's structural techniques, gives the novel a most thorough formal integrity. The book's final crystallisation is of a much profounder kind than would be suggested by Baines's view that, at best, it offers merely 'a homily against sloth'. Indeed, if one had a criticism, it might be that the ideas we shall explore in a moment are imposed on virtually every character and incident with a rigour that may seem ultimately to be too reductive of human experience.

The action of the novel begins, in one sense, when Heat is prepared to give Sir Ethelred a firm assurance that there will be no anarchist activities in London in the immediate future. After Heat's personal prestige has received something of a blow by the unexpected explosion in Greenwich Park, he will again commit himself to the view that, despite a piece of evidence which suggests otherwise, Verloc was not the instigator. Heat bases his judgements on considerable knowledge of the revolutionaries who have found a sanctuary in London, and on his own self-interest, but he cannot know of a crucial random factor: the pressure that Vladimir has applied to Verloc. Reality is far more complex and unfathomable than the certitude of one human perspective generally assumes. Throughout the novel characters will repeatedly construct hypotheses, make predictions, rest safe in complacent assumptions, only to discover the explosive unpredictability of experience.

Sometimes the blinkered response is a necessary part of the limitations of a single perspective, but often characters in *The Secret Agent* see what they want to see because their vision is narrowed by an obsessive preoccupation or ideology. For Sir Ethelred whole areas of experience are filtered through his *idée fixe* of getting through Parliament his bill for the nationalisation of fisheries; while for Ossipon, Lombroso's theories dictate glib categories of judgement. Vladimir, whose mentality is conditioned, according to Conrad, by centuries of autocracy in Russia, makes the English political scene fit in with his own preconceptions. Prejudice and the essential requirements of our temperament – 'we can never cease to be ourselves', Conrad asserts – constantly lead characters to act on mistaken premises and to form misguided judgements. Conrad's delineation of the Verloc marriage is, of course, the centrepiece of the development of this theme. The 'mistaken perspectives' that operate in this relationship have already been amply demonstrated in the commentaries on individual chapters – turn back, for instance, to the notes on Chapter 11. Winnie's whole outlook is the most extreme example of a general trait in mankind which Conrad defines in his 'Author's Note': 'the world is not interested in the motives of any overt act but in its consequences. Man may smile and smile but he is not an investigating animal. He loves the obvious. He shrinks from explanations.' Conrad the novelist *is* an 'investigating animal', and his structuring of the novel constantly moves the reader from one character's perpective to another, while his irony explores the discrepancies in judgement that are revealed. Sometimes we may share briefly the limitations of a particular character's point of view, but Conrad invites us finally to share the pleasures of his narrator's own omniscience, whereby the inherent miscalculations and weaknesses of the narrow viewpoint are transcended. As will be emphasised later in this Guide, the very structure of the novel is integral to this process, underlining the fact that any distinction between content and style – between what is said and how it is said (or revealed) – is a more than usually artificial one in the context of reading *The Secret Agent*.

4.3 SELF-INTEREST

What is it that leads to so many of the mistaken judgements we have noted? What is the essential motivation of nearly all the characters in *The Secret Agent*? Consider the springs of virtually any action or commitment in the novel. What is Conrad's diagnosis of the reason why most of the revolutionaries espouse their political cause? What is so threatened from Verloc's point of view when Vladimir makes his demand? Why does Vladimir make his demand? Why does Verloc turn to Stevie in his hour of need? What motives direct the police investigation? Why is Heat so keen to avoid implicating Verloc? And what causes the Assistant Commissioner to involve himself personally in detective work? The list of questions could be much longer; the answers to each involve many factors, but they will lead us to the discovery that, in one form or another, self-interest is the presiding deity of the novel. A world of mole-like creatures, generally driven by prejudice or appetite – it is not a congenial picture of humanity, but it is certainly the one that emerges from a reading of *The Secret Agent*.

The only characters in the novel who are not clearly motivated by egotism or self-interest are the members of Winnie's own family circle. There is a source of compassion here, although – except for Stevie – it is very narrowly focused; it is also, as a result of various forms of obtuseness, rendered inoperative – and finally turned to murderous destruction. In the case of Stevie, while he certainly responds most powerfully and widely to the suffering of others, which makes him unique in the novel, his disabled intellect means that he must remain blind to anything approaching the full complexity of its causes. He can be turned into a planter of bombs. (For a fuller discussion of Conrad's attitude to Stevie, turn to p.68.) Stevie is the sole object, of course, of Winnie's selfless devotion, but she does not understand him, a point that is made quite clear in the episode in which she accompanies him home from the almshouse; it is partly because of her dull-wittedness that their 'saviour' will turn out to be the man who destroys Stevie. The self-sacrificing action of Winnie's mother will also prove to be a serious miscalculation. The suggestion seems to be that the lack of self-interest, particularly when accompanied by the absence of insight, is not in itself a virtue. Moreover, there is perhaps something which is too purely instinctive and parochial about the self-denying actions of Winnie and her mother for them to win our unqualified approval. Even so, in the moment when Winnie realises the failure of all her deepest desires, there is a pathetic nobility in the image of the glinting of her wedding ring amid all the shabbiness of Verloc's shop. It is the glimmer of a selfless impulse that we find hardly anywhere else in *The Secret Agent*.

4.4 SOCIAL AND POLITICAL VIEWS

Conrad's experience of life at sea had no doubt caused him to feel particularly keenly the obligations of loyalty to one's fellows and of fidelity to a common purpose. The seaman's life, while offering a testing ground of the most exacting kind, also had the advantage that on most occasions its discipline and necessary toil could provide a defence against the darkness. We read, for instance, in *The Nigger of the Narcissus* (1897) that life on board ship, in its 'desired unrest', does not permit a man 'to meditate at ease upon the complicated and acrid savour of existence'. When Conrad comes to meditate on the nature of English society, his sceptical mind irresistibly finds its values riddled with indolence, purposelessness and virtually a total absence of fellow-feeling.

Conrad's deeply conservative social position springs from his pessimistic view of man's fate in the face of a chaotic universe which is no more than a 'tragic accident' (see the quotation from the letter to Cunninghame Graham on p.51). Nevertheless, although Conrad views any civilisation as an arbitrary and precarious creation of man which does not rest on any absolute values beyond him, he is prepared to discriminate between the values of one society and another. It is therefore necessary to preface the remarks that will follow with a statement that, while *The Secret Agent* offers a trenchant critique of many aspects of the institutions and values of English society, when it comes to a choice between the traditional political stability and essential commitment to legality – with all its complacent weaknesses – that Conrad found in English life and the alternative offered by the vicious Vladimir, there is no question where Conrad stands.

The aspects of English society that attract Conrad's highly sceptical attention in the novel include its government, its police, its aristocracy – and the institution of marriage. There is more than a suggestion that the 'respectability' and conventional stabilities, domestic and public, that prevail among the English populace derive from a combination of stolidity and, as we have already discussed, an all-pervasive, self-interested morality. The descriptions of London throughout the novel reveal a stultifying drabness; most of the city's citizens exist in a kind of torpor. Yet, in Chapter 8, for instance, in the description of the journey in the hackney carriage to the almshouse, there is abundant evidence as to why, to anybody of a sensitive, responsive spirit, the very streets of this part of London might arouse a fierce indignation; there is a lifeless impoverishment which appears to cry out for remedy. It seems 'the height of positive wickedness' for the profusion of gas lights to illuminate this death-in-life squalor. In the lot of the emaciated horse, a 'steed of apocalyptic misery', and its driver we may find a cameo of the way in which hardship is passed on from man to man – and to beast – and a hopeless assessment that the unjust nature of existence, by an inhuman necessity, compels the subjugated to intensify the pain of those just below them in a hierarchy of suffering. In the deepest sense, it is all indeed a 'shame'. Yet Conrad himself believes this state of things derives from the nature of man's universal condition: it is not to be softened or solved by Stevie's wish to take the cabhorse to bed – or by any tinkering with social legislation or any profound revolutionary sweeping away of the corruption that offends.

Conrad knows, however, that the seedbed for violent revolution is present in those streets through which the 'Cab of Death' passes. Stevie represents an extreme example of a type in whom an acute awareness of and responsiveness to suffering and injustice are combined with an exaggerated inability to grapple intellectually with the whole nexus of factors involved in man's condition; it is a mentality which exposes this kind of temperament, in Conrad's view, to the fraudulent, glib response of revolutionary or anarchist ideology, by means of which are exploited 'the poignant miseries and passionate credulities of a mankind always so tragically eager for self-destruction' (see the 'Author's Note').

Those in positions of power, from Heat, who has no understanding at all of the impulses that might produce an anarchist, to Sir Ethelred, are apparently insulated from any sense of the dangers that are latent in these oppressive and abundant miseries. It is not that Conrad is suggesting that English society is becoming dangerously unstable or in the immediate future is moving towards some pre-revolutionary state – the apathetic crowds that so dispirit the Professor seem to rule out that possibility – but Conrad does accuse the English of a terrible complacency. Sir Ethelred's blinkered preoccupation with his nationalisation of fisheries bill is just one gauge of this complacency.

Conrad himself does not have so much a political position as an immense scepticism about all political commitments. If a political opinion emerges from *The Secret Agent*, it is a sense that perhaps in Conrad's view it is both a strength and a weakness of those who manage English social and political institutions that they take for granted a kind of inevitable permanence and continuity – remember the myopic assumptions of Michaelis's patroness – whereas Conrad's own early experience of a different kind of society in Poland under the Russians had given him a profound awareness that, to a greater or lesser extent, all societies exist precariously on the edge of a dark abyss.

4.5 SCIENCE

Conrad dedicated *The Secret Agent* to H. G. Wells (1866–1946), who as well as being a prolific novelist, a pioneer of science fiction and a social reformer was one of the most influential popul250ers of science of the age. There was a strong streak of pessimism in Wells, but his public posture was generally that of an advocate of the progress that was to be brought about by a combination of socialism and the application of science to the problems of society. When Wells championed Conrad's early writing, Conrad was grateful. In return he valued certain aspects of Wells's work, though it is significant that the dedication to *The Secret Agent* specifies Wells's imaginative writing rather than current polemical works such as *A Modern Utopia* (1905), for Conrad undoubtedly had the strongest reservations about many of Wells's radical social views and his scientific emphasis. It is interesting to note that after the appearance of *The Secret Agent* the friendship between Conrad and Wells seems to have cooled considerably. One likely reason for this is that, despite the ostensibly warm tone of the novel's dedication, Wells recognised that in *The Secret Agent* Conrad was, among other matters, unmistakably offering a corrective to the Wellsian gospel of what the advancement of science had to offer.

Conrad defined the essential difference between Wells and himself as follows: 'You don't care for humanity but think they are to be improved. I love humanity but know that they are not!' For Conrad, much of what was called science in his day had about the same significance as a game played with luminous dominoes in the dark, and one aspect of his attitude towards science is expressed in satirical fashion by Vladimir – on a rare occasion when the views of the author and this cynical manipulator coincide for a moment. After Vladimir has lectured Verloc on the way in which science in the present age has assumed an importance in the popular mind which far outweighs that of, for instance, art or religion, Vladimir observes that every worthy citizen seems to believe that, in some vague way, his own material interests and the progress of society in general are largely dependent on science. It is because science has become a 'sacrosanct fetish' that Vladimir feels his plan to strike a blow against one of its most abstract manifestations will be so singularly shocking to popular feeling. A bomb outrage at the Greenwich Observatory may also, Vladimir calculates, outrage the scientific establishment: 'All the damned professors are radicals at heart. Let them know that their great panjandrum has got to go, too, to make room for the Future of the Proletariat.'

The thrust behind this remark by Vladimir is the implication that the pairing of radical political policies and the advancement of science as the two supreme initiators of beneficial social change ought to be more sceptically considered. Conrad is suggesting that Wells and other scientific utopians should recognise that many of their revolutionary comrades have no respect at all for science – that is, science defined as the unconstrained pursuit of empirical knowledge by the free-ranging intellects of its practitioners. The Professor's vision of the future, for instance, would sweep away all science of that kind, along with all the other disinterested pursuits of liberal humanism. Conrad asserts, as Orwell was later to foretell in *Nineteen Eighty-Four*, that it is a nonsense to believe that the unfettered science of the free, enquiring mind that Wells values would remain sacrosanct in a revolutionary scenario of the future. To imagine that the scientific intellectual will somehow occupy a specially protected area during and after the social cataclysm is to be as blind to the actual dynamics of revolutionary politics as Michaelis's patroness.

In *The Secret Agent* it is also a part of Conrad's reactionary case against science – or, at least, against a complacent belief in science as a universal panacea – that, of itself, science can generate no sustaining moral values. This view is certainly borne out when we consider the two 'representatives' of science in the novel, the Professor and Ossipon; though it is worth remembering that both characters have largely been failures in their respective spheres and that what they offer is scientism rather than science. Yet the Professor's motto of 'Exterminate, exterminate!' represents a violent and grim version of a kind of social Darwinism in which the fittest, a master race, survive because of their preternatural viciousness. There is a fascism of mathematical precision behind the Professor's scenario for the future which subverts the dreams of a scientific utopian: 'First the great multitude of the weak must go, then the only relatively strong. You see? First the blind, then the deaf and the dumb, then the halt and the lame – and so on . . . I remain – if I am strong enough.' Indeed, the Professor's hatred of his fellow men may be seen as an extreme satirical distortion of Wells's own outlook, which despite a *general* humanitarian appeal also contained elements of a mandarin disdain for the unintelligent masses. (Remember Conrad's assertion: 'You don't care for humanity'.)

The Professor's obsession with the 'pure' technical problem of devising the perfect detonator may seem to represent one aspect of scientific detachment, but the essential motivation – as is the case with his whole ideology of destruction – springs from personal weakness and grievance. Unlike Wells, who had 'made good' from a humble beginning, the Professor has not gained the social recognition which he feels his genius deserves. His attitude that someone – society at large – must pay for this state of affairs is simply a more sophisticated (and selfish) version of Stevie's automatic response which is then dressed up as dogma. In Ossipon's case, too, we may see how values which are alleged to be 'scientific' and disinterested are, in fact, no more than an extension of self-interest and temperamental need. When Ossipon, 'free from the restraints of conventional morality', rejects Winnie's cry for help and consigns her to the darkness, he attempts to maintain a clinical detachment from her: do not the theories of Lombroso entirely justify his rejection of a woman who clearly bears the same deterministic signs of degeneracy as were visible in her brother, Stevie? There is, of course, no kind of scientific disinterestedness here. But the main issue is not simply the glibness and spuriousness of Lombroso's theories; it is rather the motivation of moral shallowness in Ossipon, for whom the adoption of these theories has always been, at bottom, an evasion of individual responsibility. (It is, incidentally, one of Conrad's little jokes that he endows Ossipon with the physical characteristics which, according to Lombroso, denoted a cheat and a violator of women: the robust anarchist obviously cannot see his own face in the mirror!) What Ossipon clings to in Lombroso is merely another of those simplifying patterns that Conrad suggests humankind inveterately seeks to impose on the irreducible complexities of experience. Even though Ossipon in his shocked state of mind at the end of the novel is still to be heard declaring that 'science reigns already', even though he still prattles on about a brave new world ruled over by doctors of science, in his dark heart personal guilt works remorselessly, and there Lombroso can offer no final defence.

4.6 TIME

Time is a major preoccupation in the novel, as the following list of examples will confirm:

1. After his interview with Vladimir in Chapter 2, Verloc, absorbed by his anxiety, finds himself back at Brett Street 'as borne from west to east on the wings of a great wind'. This contrasts with the leisurely, drawn-out nature of his journey to the embassy.

2. Towards the end of Chapter 3, the 'drowsy ticking of the old clock' on the landing outside the Verlocs' bedroom is heard marking off the seconds between the couple's desultory scraps of conversation; while

for Verloc, facing another sleepless night, the steps of a passer-by in the street seem to 'pace out all eternity'. Again at the end of Chapter 8, we will hear the same clock counting off 'fifteen ticks into the abyss of eternity' before Winnie puts out the light.

3. In Chapter 4, Ossipon is filled with dread at the thought of the twenty seconds it would take from the Professor's squeezing of the detonator to the explosion of his portable bomb.

4. Heat feels it is possible that the victim of the bomb in Greenwich Park, in the split second before his death, passed through the pangs of 'inconceivable pain', and by questioning the idea of 'instantaneous' death, the narrator comments that Heat rose above 'the vulgar conception of time'.

5. The limited amount of time that Sir Ethelred can spare the Assistant Commissioner is emphasised throughout their discussion. In Chapter 7, while the Assistant Commissioner speaks, 'the hands of the face of the clock behind the great man's back . . . with a ghostly evanescent tick – had moved through the space of seven minutes'.

6. During the journey to the almshouse in Chapter 8, there are moments when time and motion, as perceived from inside the cab, seem to come to a complete stop. This sense of stasis is produced because of the absence of 'visual evidences' outside the cab which would normally mark off the sense of movement: 'the effect was of being shaken in a stationary apparatus'.

7. At the end of the Assistant Commissioner's full and productive evening – see the close of Chapter 10 – so much has been packed into a relatively short space of time that he is surprised when his watch indicates that it is only half past ten.

8. In the instant before the carving knife plunges into Verloc's breast, the moment is described in a kind of slow-motion (Chapter 11). Verloc, in a split second, has the impression that he can conceive of a plan of escape as he tastes 'the flavour of death rising in his gorge'. In fact, he has time to move neither hand nor foot.

9. After the murder, the drops of blood fall on the floorcloth 'with a sound of ticking growing fast and furious like the pulse of an insane clock'. It is a sound which brings Winnie back to reality and to an appreciation of the horror of what she has done. When Winnie is

about to leave the house after the murder, she cannot believe that only two minutes have elapsed since she last looked at the clock. She wonders whether, as in those tales from folklore, the clock had stopped at the moment of the murder. The narrator comments that 'as a matter of fact, only three minutes had elapsed from the moment she had drawn the first deep, easy breath after the blow, to this moment'.

10. During the description leading up to the departure of the 10.30 train from Waterloo in the final chapter, the narrator keeps us very carefully informed about the time that remains. In the final moments, Ossipon looks at Winnie 'with a sort of medical air as if counting the seconds'. And after his carefully timed leap from the train, he walks the town to hear the hours chiming above his head: 'Half past twelve of a wild night in the Channel. . .'

It should be clear enough from these examples that there are two concepts of time in the novel. Certainly time may be measured as simply a sequence of equally spaced moments, but the intensity of individual response will also create its own separate sense of the temporal. Time as it is actually perceived may appear to move quickly, slowly, or even stand still. The novel stresses the relativity of time – as well as that of truth.

Once again we will see how this thematic concern links with the structure of the novel. A chronological thread ties all the events together, and the exact spacing of episodes in a temporal sequence – for instance, Ossipon arriving precisely when he does at Verloc's shop in Chapter 12 – often suggests something close to the workings of fate; but the novel's time-scheme fluidly follows the pattern of the narrator's 'investigation'. The structure of the novel creates 'holes in time' which will be filled in later; it can move backwards and forwards in time to locate the critical episodes in a pattern which is to be judged finally by intensity and significance of experience, rather than the ticking of seconds. However, there are ubiquitous reminders in the novel that those seconds are always ticking away 'into the abyss of eternity', a fact which is another gauge of Conrad's assessment of the transitory nature of man's existence.

5 CHARACTERISATION

The depth of characterisation in the novel varies. Verloc and Winnie are conceived in terms of a fairly limited palette but, because they are placed in a number of different situations in the narrative and viewed from a range of perspectives, they acquire a certain depth. At the other extreme, there are portraits which are intentionally conceived by the author as caricatures. Figures such as Karl Yundt or Sir Ethelred exist in two dimensions only. A number of other characters – Winnie's mother, the Assistant Commissioner and Michaelis's patroness – are not even given a personal name, as if a simple designation defines sufficiently their essence and function. This kind of implicit reduction of human beings to the status of the barest kind of nomenclature is also expressed through the epithets attached repeatedly to the revolutionary characters: Michaelis, the 'ticket-of-leave apostle', or Ossipon, 'the robust anarchist', or Karl Yundt, 'the terrorist', are descriptions which quickly take on the ring of withering scorn.

Perhaps one key element to an understanding of the characterisation in *The Secret Agent* is to observe the patterning produced by the different manifestations in each character of what seems like an epidemical self-interest and capacity for misjudgement. We should also note the effect of the grooves of convention and routine, and the way virtually every character attempts to negotiate for him- or herself the kind of existence which seems to be adjusted to deep-seated temperamental needs. The narrator of *Under Western Eyes* (1911) observes that all men in one way or another seek 'some form or perhaps only some formula of peace'. It is a comment that might usefully be applied to the characters we meet in *The Secret Agent*.

For convenience of discussion the main characters have been divided into three groups.

5.1 THE VERLOC HOUSEHOLD

Verloc and Winnie

Much has already been written in this Guide about the characters of Verloc and Winnie. What will be emphasised in this section is the extent to which the *tone* of Conrad's prose embodies his attitude towards character. Consider the manner in which the narrator introduces us to Verloc:

> His eyes were naturally heavy; he had an air of having wallowed, fully dressed, all day on an unmade bed. Another man would have felt such an appearance a distinct disadvantage. In a commercial transaction of the retail order much depends on the seller's engaging and amiable aspect. But Mr Verloc knew his business, and remained undisturbed by any sort of aesthetic doubt about his appearance.

Already, of course, Conrad's irony is playing around the nature of Verloc's real business: a certain seediness of appearance perhaps nicely matches the kind of goods on sale in Verloc's shop – but then we will soon learn that Verloc's livelihood does not depend on any need to ingratiate himself with his customers. The tone of the prose – and it strikes the keynote of the narrator's attitude to the secret agent – is one of amused derision. Right from the start the reader feels that Verloc is held firmly between the tweezers of the author's sardonic mockery. This is a narrator who is so assured in his judgement that, by the use of a knowingly inflated precision of diction and syntax, he may sometimes pontificate and generalise in a way that is calculated both to amuse the reader and to alert him or her to share an attitude of contempt. To write, for instance, that Verloc 'remained undisturbed by any sort of aesthetic doubt about his appearance' is to appear to dignify Verloc with this portentous register of language while, because of its manifest inappropriateness, allowing the incongruity of the tone to score a satirical point against the lazy, untidy and disreputable man who is so described.

An implicit note of bathos is continually present in Conrad's treatment of Verloc; he relishes cutting this character down to size. Indeed, Verloc is the source of much of the best humour in the novel: for instance, shortly after the description quoted above, note the deflating simile which celebrates Verloc's return to London: '(like the influenza) from the Continent, only he arrived unheralded by the Press'. Verloc is not only to be thought of in terms of an infectious disease; we will also register the reference to his physical appearance – he looks as if he has 'wallowed' on an unmade bed – which, as well as insinuating a point about the indolent and irregular nature of his existence, brings to mind a pig in a sty. It is a parallel that the narrator implicitly develops. Verloc has grown fat off his easy life, a point Vladimir maliciously underlines: 'He's fat – the animal'. Moreover, in Verloc's self-satisfaction, his eating habits, his lusts – and even in the way he dies, stuck like a pig – there is something suggestively porcine. When the narrator bids farewell to this adipose mediocrity, it is with an appropriately ironic epitaph which, in its wryly sententious accumulation of epithets and mock-heroic tone, perfectly signals his amused contempt for Verloc's pretensions:

Night, the inevitable reward of men's faithful labours on this earth, night had fallen on Mr Verloc, the tried revolutionist – 'one of the old lot' – the humble guardian of society; the invaluable secret agent △ of Baron Stott-Wartenheim's dispatches; a servant of law and order, faithful, trusted, accurate, admirable. . .

The author's attitude to Winnie is rather more complex. Conrad has sometimes been accused of being less than successful in the portrayal of women in his novels; the claim has even been made that he is a misogynist. However, it is worth remembering that in his 'Author's Note' Conrad tells us that the conception of Winnie's character was central to the whole novel. For most readers she finally ceases to be a mere caricature of incuriosity and inspires some genuine pathos. The image of the ring that glints in Verloc's shop grimly underlines the futility of Winnie's self-sacrifice – it is like some treasured jewel 'dropped in a dust-bin' – and it is true that both life and death were mysteries for poor Winnie. Yet in the account of her suicide, through what may seem at first the mere superficialities and clichés of a newspaper report, there is the creation of a haunting undertone which makes us imagine her final, tortured state of mind. Certain phrases from the newspaper cutting are burned into Ossipon's mind; they will also trigger in the reader a disproportionate amount of feeling which goes far beyond the denotative meaning of a few threadbare phrases. For instance, the very expression 'hang for ever' evokes something of Winnie's final terror by reminding us of her hysterical fear of the drop of fourteen feet. Like Ossipon, we fill in the blanks that lie behind the barest details which record something of what was observed of Winnie on the Channel crossing. The fate to which Ossipon exposed her involves focusing on an image of Winnie without money, without hope, without any saviour – and without Stevie. Totally alone, she faced that darkness. And entered it.

Winnie's death, which occurs 'off stage', provides the most moving episode of the whole novel. Her fate is not subjected to the kind of heavy irony with which the narrator marked Verloc's exit from the narrative. Indeed, in the very *withdrawal* of the narrator's voice – the scourge of so many characters in the novel – and in the tactful registering of Winnie's death through the carefully arranged fragments of a newspaper account, there is a reticence which marks one of the few acts of authorial compassion in the whole of *The Secret Agent*.

Stevie

One can see how easily Stevie might have been sentimentalised. Surrounded by the self-interested, he might have played the role of the 'noble fool' – the Romantic stereotype of the great-souled idiot boy, sensitive and full of a human sympathy which responds to suffering in a direct way far beyond the capacity of the sane and sophisticated. Conrad is too clear-sighted, too sceptical, too morally aware to adopt this approach. Stevie's feelings are genuine enough, but Conrad is at pains to emphasise that *simply* to feel deeply about injustice is not to provide a solution. Stevie wants the cabman to stop whipping the horse; the cabman's words to him are of central importance: 'This ain't an easy world.' What about the cabman's lot? And his responsibilities? Faced with the notion that merely to stop whipping the horse will not begin to meet the complexity of the causes of human misery, Stevie can only retreat into impotent violence and vindictiveness. Conrad wishes us to see Stevie's welter of blind, passionate emotion, which has nowhere to go until Verloc points the direction, as positively dangerous. Warm-heartedness and weak-headedness is a combination Conrad cannot recommend (the minor story 'The Anarchist' is instructive on this point) and the sadness of Stevie's plight is that because of his mental weakness he is unusually vulnerable – not least to his own feelings – and impressionable. Conrad's treatment of Stevie, however, ensures that we are largely detached from his suffering when he is manipulated into following a futilely self-destructive destiny.

5.2 THE REVOLUTIONARIES

Except for the Professor, perhaps, the revolutionary characters are two-dimensional figures and totally ineffectual. This is probably why we feel a shade uncomfortable in the presence of Ossipon's guilt at the end of the novel, for the shallowness of his portrayal has previously suggested that, as is the case with all his associates, moral awareness is beyond his compass. Conrad knows that there are some revolutionaries who are motivated by an acute sense of the inequalities and corruptions of existing society and a sincere desire to remedy them. Conrad concedes this motivation to some of the more fully drawn characters we meet in the later novel, *Under Western Eyes* (1911); but even a misguided idealism is a quality almost entirely missing from the 'sham' revolutionists of *The Secret Agent*. Conrad gives his harsh diagnosis of their 'revolutionary' motivation in Chapter 3. It springs, he suggests, from a rejection of any kind of recognised labour: 'For obviously one does not revolt against the advantages of that state, but against the price which must be paid for the same in the coin of accepted morality, and toil. The majority of revolutionists are the enemies of discipline and fatigue.'

When Conrad was accused of reactionary bias in the novel, his reply was simple, though perhaps a shade disingenuous: 'I don't think I've been satirising the revolutionary world. All these people are not revolutionaries – they are shams . . . I hope you have seen that the purpose of my book was *not* to attack any doctrine, or even the men holding that doctrine.' However that may be, Conrad certainly is eager to stress that the spring of the revolutionary ideology of an Ossipon is to be found in temperamental weakness and a desire to get by without undue exertion. Ossipon may parade an antagonistic stance towards society, but his practical impulse is to preserve a cosy niche for himself in the existing social structure. Like Michaelis, he has a vested interest in the *status quo*. Note, for instance, Ossipon's reaction when he first hears of the news of the explosion in Greenwich Park: 'the even tenor of his revolutionary life was menaced by no fault of his own'. His first thought is that this untimely outrage may lead to the cutting of his 'modest subsidy' as editor of the F. P. pamphlets. The irony of Conrad's comment is expressed through the juxtaposition of 'even tenor' and 'revolutionary life'.

Conrad did not believe that a man generally sits down and, in a disinterested, cerebral fashion, chooses the political and social principles he will espouse. What a man may call an 'ideology', Conrad suggests, is invariably an extension of that man's essential emotional requirements; it is a product of temperament, prejudice and previous experience of life. We are told in the novel that 'the way of even the most justifiable revolutions is prepared by *personal impulses disguised into creeds*' (my italics). The characters of Michaelis, Yundt, Ossipon and even the Professor may be seen as case histories which underpin this judgement. Yundt, a character who really has no part to play in the novel's plot, is by nature a sadist, though a premature senility has curtailed the acting out of his violent fantasies. His zeal to urge on a band of young destroyers who will pitilessly tear apart the rotting carcass of society clearly derives from this singularly repulsive trait. At the other extreme, Michaelis's quietist faith in a utopia that will result from the interplay of economic forces – and without, therefore, the need for any concerted action on his part – exactly answers the requirements of his own flaccid passivity. Moreover, Conrad points up the fact that his vision of the future was formed during his long years in prison – in complete isolation from the corrective value of most people's everyday experience. There he founded a faith that will remain unmoved by argument or the troublesome complexities of life. He has discovered his formula of peace.

The Professor is in a different category. He will strike us as a much more serious proposition as a revolutionary than any of Verloc's associates we see at Brett Street. He has a purpose of deadly destructiveness. He has no moral scruples. His life possesses an ascetic dedication. He knows that one of the first steps to producing anomie is to undermine society's belief in legality. He points out to Ossipon that the habits of mind of Ossipon and his colleagues are in reality all of a piece with the values of the society they imagine that they challenge. In contrast, the Professor's extreme form of anarchism is devoted to the end of destroying the whole edifice of society with no thought of what will replace it – except the assurance that the strong annihilators will inherit this world. His moral nihilism, active policy – he is making and supplying bombs while the other revolutionists merely talk about theory – and his preparedness to sacrifice his own life undoubtedly give him a chilling intensity. Yet at the same time his ideology and self-assertion mask an essential weakness of character; his paranoia, mediocrity and sense of failure are bolstered up by his arrogant assumption of the role of the destroying avenger. Even he suspects in his more desperate moments that his final weapon of terror will simply shatter ineffectively against the 'unattackable stolidity' of heedless mankind.

5.3 THE PUBLIC DOMAIN

Heat and the Assistant Commissioner

Conrad to some extent balances his indictment of the revolutionary mentality with an almost equally sceptical examination of certain aspects of the police investigation. Heat, ploddingly effective as his past services to the Special Crime branch have shown him to be – though much of his prestige rests on the covert use of Verloc as an informant – is caught off guard by the Greenwich affair. The narrator's irony leaves in tatters any claim that Heat is working solely for the 'good of society'. Since in his efforts to control revolutionary activity there are few accepted 'rules', his practice is to make up his own. He has no scruples over the suppression of evidence, if it suits his purposes; he also assumes the right to connive with criminals and to choose his own time for the arrest of a guilty man. His approach to the Greenwich investigation reveals in a particularly naked way the wrong-headedness of his methods and the extent to which they are governed by a brazen self-interest.

Heat will never know the extent to which what he sees as the Assistant Commissioner's bungling interference in his delicately poised 'game' is also the result of self-serving motives. This intelligent man has found the sustaining centre to his present uncongenial life in an impersonal ritual of daily whist, played at his Club with 'co-sufferers . . . as if it were indeed a drug against the secret ills of existence'. It is just as important to the Assistant Commissioner as it is to Verloc, in another context, that the boat of his marital compromise, which contains a difficult wife, should not be rocked. In the defence of his formula of peace, the Assistant Commissioner rejoices in a return to his earlier colonial role as a lone wolf. The urbane official whose name in private life we never learn, the gentleman who can handle Sir Ethelred or Michaelis's patroness with such tactical skill, is happiest when he breaks free of his desk-bound role. (There may be some sympathetic identification here on the part of Conrad, the novelist, former seaman and adventurer.) Behind the coldly bureaucratic designation lies the stifled spirit of a man of action who seeks to attain a kind of protean vitality in the acting out of a number of identities and roles, and in the setting of a novel which abounds in characters who exist inertly in a fixed state, this quality gives him a striking energy and interest. Before his visit to Brett Street we see the Assistant Commissioner slipping on the rather romantic persona of a 'cool, reflective Don Quixote'. With boyish relish he assumes a disguise which bestows on him an insalubrious 'foreignness', and a feeling of 'evil freedom'. In the drab streets around Verloc's shop he looks 'as though he were a member of the criminal classes'. Despite all of this, the same thread of self-interest runs through the whole gamut of his roles, and he is instantly identified by Heat when Winnie supplies the Inspector with the merest scraps of a description. The Assistant Commissioner, like everyone else in the novel, has never ceased to be himself.

Sir Ethelred
In contrast to an apparently multifarious quality in the portrayal of the Assistant Commissioner, Sir Ethelred is delineated – in a similar fashion to revolutionists such as Michaelis and Yundt – as virtually a two-dimensional caricature. Conrad's attitude to Sir Ethelred is interesting. The author may nod with a degree of respect in the direction of the great man's pedigree – he belongs to an elite accustomed to the burdens of political power – and to the facts that, unlike the anarchists, he works very hard and seeks to bring about his 'revolutionary' reforms through constitutional channels. It is when we ask exactly where Sir Ethelred's prodigious efforts are directed and what motives lead him to grant a ready ear to the Assistant Commissioner, that the chivalric connotations of his name will ring with a teasing irony. Sir Ethelred's obsession with the nationalisation of the fisheries – a footling and misguided piece of legislation according to Conrad's own political susceptibilities – and the fact that he can spare only a few minutes to deal with the problem of an anarchist outrage, do rather suggest a certain putting of the cart before the horse. With an odd tunnel vision, the Secretary of State sees the Special Crimes branch's surveillance of revolutionaries largely as a technical means to an end. For reasons of his own political interest as a radical minister, he does not not want to run the risk of a reactionary backlash. That was, from the first, his concern when he sought the original assurance from Heat. It is an odd sense of priorities which gives such inordinate importance to the passing of his bill on the fisheries. If Chief Inspector Heat is hide-bound by the rules of the game he plays, Sir Ethelred is equally tied up in what Conrad views as petty political strategems and superficialities. Of course, the caustic scorn which Conrad directs at the anarchists is absent here, but nevertheless Sir Ethelred's portrait is satirical in a playfully farcical way – an impression that is underlined by the keeper of the gate, Toodles, who ushers us into the great man's presence with such awed puerility.

Vladimir
Conrad's attitude to the cynical and manipulative Vladimir is highly critical. Behind the diplomat's façade of refined dress and manners, Conrad intimates that the man is a barbarian. Vladimir has a contempt for English tolerance, flexibility and restraint, qualities he views merely as showing 'sentimental regard for individual liberty'. He thrives on the politics of confrontation; he wishes to polarise attitudes. In Chapter 2, he outlines his scheme to Verloc with apparent intellectual detachment, but his interpretation of political

reality – as Verloc angrily realises – is highly contradictory. For instance, at one moment he will speak of Verloc's revolutionary associates who have found refuge in London as though they were a gang of idle incompetents (which they are), and at the next as though he really believes his own scaremongering propaganda that these men pose a serious threat to the whole structure of society. When we find Vladimir off his home ground and are able to view him from a different perspective in Chapter 10, we shall see clearly revealed the insecurity and weakness behind his urbane mask as, his guilt speedily discovered, the political assumptions of the autocrat are subjected to the Assistant Commissioner's sceptical mockery.

6 TECHNICAL FEATURES

6.1 NARRATIVE STRUCTURE

Because Conrad is profoundly aware that there is an apparently unfathomable depth to most areas of human experience, as a novelist he is perhaps preoccupied to an unusual degree with the way in which a narrative is to be structured in order to penetrate through to its mysterious essence. In some of Conrad's fiction the use of a narrative in the first person offered a solution. Conrad uses Marlow in this role on a number of occasions: in *Heart of Darkness* (1902) it is this character who links the 'frame' of the tale – the quotidian reality of the four men, united by the 'bond of the sea', who sit on the deck of a ship on the Thames waiting for the tide to turn – with the elusive, haunted nature of a narrative which describes Marlow's confrontation with the darkness of the Congo – and with Kurtz. Even so, Marlow will sometimes break off from his account which deals with experience 'on the stretch', exasperated by the difficulty of communicating the essence of his story to listeners who are necessarily limited by the perspectives of everyday reality: 'Do you see the story? Do you see anything? It seems to me I am trying to tell you a dream. . . No, it is impossible; it is impossible to convey the life sensation of any given epoch of one's experience – that which makes its truth, its meaning – its subtle and penetrating essence.'

In *The Secret Agent* Conrad uses an *omniscient narrator*, that is a narrator who writes of events in the third person; the reader accepts the convention that the author has a free hand to switch the narrative focus from one character to the next, to take the reader at will inside the mind of every one of his creations, and to shift the setting of the narrative as the author deems necessary. In *The Secret Agent* a narrator of singularly lofty omniscience is required to reveal the essential heart of the narrative with the kind of ironic detachment that Conrad was seeking. The structure of the novel, with its extensive use of switches in perspective and time, embodies Conrad's emphasis on the relativity of truth (and also of time) by making us view events from the standpoint of a particular character at a specific moment, only to reveal the ironic disparity between the 'reality' the character has created in his own mind and that which is available to us through the eyes of the all-seeing narrator. The reader is placed finally in a position very close to omniscience, but at various points in the narrative we are made to share initially some of the limitations of perspective that beset the characters in the novel to such a peculiar degree. In Chapter 4, for instance, we will probably accept, with some reservations, Ossipon's view of who was killed by the explosion in Greenwich Park. By the time Ossipon arrives at Brett Street in Chapter 12, we will be in a god-like position of being able to appreciate the ludicrous nature of Ossipon's misconception. The narrative structure of the novel enforces on the reader that what characters consider the truth is invariably only a selected and highly partial version of it, coloured by their obtuseness, self-interest, automatic routines or the inevitable limitations of one single perspective. Characters' lives in *The Secret Agent* are based upon selected fictions. The novel asserts that it is only by joining together a number of different perspectives that we may approach the elusive nature of truth.

The way in which Conrad dovetails into position the various points of view and episodes in a shifting sequence of time repays close study. Consider, for instance, one aspect of how this is done in Chapter 9. Almost casually, the narrator has moved events to the day of the fatal episode in Greenwich Park, and when we see the Assistant Commissioner enter Verloc's shop we will be aware that this extends one arc of time which, temporarily suspended at the end of Chapter 7, now intersects with another sweep of the novel's time-sequence. The alert reader may also remember the close of Chapter 4, and be anticipating the arrival at this same location of Comrade Ossipon. As well as displaying for our inspection a whole range of ironies, the time-scheme the novel adopts suggests that 'reality' is to be perceived not simply as *one* story that unfolds chronologically; rather we must develop a sense of the way in which widely separated areas of temporal experience relate to and impinge upon each other. Many chapters in the novel move with a painstaking, extended deliberation to locate characters in what seem to be discrete spheres of time and space. Chapter 9 might appear at first glance to be packed with several disjointed episodes. In fact, the thread of Winnie's journey to painful enlightenment unifies each element as we see, mainly through her eyes, Verloc's state of shock (she thinks her husband is sickening for a cold), the arrival of the 'stranger' we know to be the Assistant Commissioner hot on Verloc's trail, and then the appalling *dénouement* of her conversation with Heat. This series of entrances and exits we observe on the stage of the Verloc's shop, each one heralded by the bell's mock-portentous 'crack of doom', has been prepared for by the narrator in the most meticulous fashion. The final effect of the novel's structure encourages us to imagine the experience of characters as a series of distinct lines which generally run collaterally but which will occasionally intersect to produce significant, or even climactic, results. This structure embodies, therefore, a sense of both the essential separateness of characters' experience – and its simultaneity.

6.2 IRONY

The narrative structure of the novel is integrally related to Conrad's ironic treatment of his material. Irony, of course, depends on the reader's being placed in the privileged position of knowing more about a situation than at least one of the characters involved in it. To appreciate irony we have to be in possession of the information which allows us to perceive the strange interplay between appearance and reality; more particularly, to see the ironic implications of a word or action, we need to be aware of the background situation which has led to a character's statement and/or the consequences that an action produces. It is therefore usual for the possibilities for dramatic irony to become richer as the action of a literary work develops. So, for instance, at the simplest level, the full irony of Lear's 'I shall go mad' spoken fairly early in Shakespeare's play may escape us the first time we see the play; we really need to have the prior knowledge of what fate lies in store for Lear to respond to the ironic resonance of the line in its context; it is, if you like, a 'foreshadowing irony'. There are certainly many 'foreshadowing ironies' in *The Secret Agent*, and the purpose of this rather facile comparison is not to suggest that Conrad is a superior ironist to Shakespare but that Conrad's method of narration, with its use of switches in time, location and perspective, is peculiarly adapted to present ironies for our detailed inspection, because it often presents us with the consequences of an action *before* we see that action described in full detail. To give some concrete force to this rather abstract idea, consider, for instance, the treatment of Verloc's planning of the planting of the bomb in Greenwich Park.

By the time we reach the beginning of Chapter 8, the reader will have formed the judgement that Ossipon's assumption is wrong: it was poor Stevie who was the victim of the explosion. By moving the narrative backwards, as it were, at this point, Conrad allows us to appreciate – in the dramatic 'present' as the action unfolds – the incongruous combination of motives and events which led up to the consequence of Stevie's demise. This produces a situation fraught with irony, most of which derives from Winnie's blindness; unlike Winnie, the reader has a fairly clear-sighted view of the background to Verloc's behaviour and of what the future holds for Stevie. There is the 'situational irony' of Winnie's self-congratulation in Chapter 9 as she sees her husband and Stevie going off for their walks: 'Mr Verloc seemed to be taking kindly to Stevie's companionship'. There are also verbal ironies which take on a sinisterly comic ring: Winnie assures Verloc that Stevie 'would go through fire for you'.

It must be recognised that Conrad's use of irony is not the application of some mere cosmetic which is smoothed over the surface of the narrative. In the 'Author's Note' to the novel, Conrad tells us that an ironic method of dealing with his subject was 'formulated with deliberation and in the earnest belief that ironic treatment alone would enable me to say all that I felt I would have to say in scorn as well as in pity'. Conrad was aware that his narrative contains much potentially melodramatic material. There is the background of political intrigue and anarchist activity (and inactivity); a bomb outrage which leads to a police investigation and to repercussions in the corridors of power; and the novel concludes with a domestic murder and a suicide. Sensational stuff! But it is not so in Conrad's treatment of events. He will use suspense, and even tantalise the reader by the dangling of clues; he wants the reader to become engaged in the narrative, but not solely on an emotional level. His ironic approach, linked with the tone of the prose, makes the reader keep his or her distance. We are seldom invited to identify with the characters; the ironies which underpin the narrative invite exploration and moral judgement.

So, ironies of the kind we noted in Chapter 9, far from producing merely a series of ironic flashes, illuminate a whole calculated method of investigation. Irony is a tool for moral discrimination; by means of irony Conrad underlines the culpability of characters who are wilfully obtuse or blinded by their self-interested point of view. Yet, as no single character, in the widest terms of the novel, can 'know everything', it is through irony that Conrad suggests a whole world-view. It is a deeply pessimistic one. Not only do characters prefer not to think about the complexities and incongruities of their true situation; it is also evident that the control they believe they have over their own destiny is limited – perhaps even totally illusory.

Conrad's ironic method shows that while a singular incuriosity *is* responsible for much of Winnie's suffering, even the most percipient of characters can never judge truly the full consequences of their actions. Winnie's fate borders on the tragic, and indeed many of the ironies in the novel have a sombre undertone; yet their total effect is not one which necessarily induces gloom. It is with a finally omniscient, remote detachment that we see the coupling of the ironic links in the narrative which fetter characters to the consequences of their actions that they are unable to understand or control, not only as a result of constitutional obtuseness but also because it is in the very nature of things, Conrad asserts, for human beings to be blind. From this final perspective, which is enforced by the narrator's loftily magisterial prose style, the ultimate vision of the novel is a comic one. To witness this drama, which is played out mainly by mediocrities, from a god's eye view, and to be made emotionally distant from it, is to be given a licence to smile, albeit wryly.

6.3 CONRAD'S NARRATOR

At numerous stages in this Guide references have been made to the 'narrator' or to the 'author', rather than directly to Conrad. This distinction, while it has not been maintained with any rigorous consistency, *is* an important one. The role of the author is, of course, an extension of Conrad's everyday self, but, just as clearly, the authorial presence that dominates *The Secret Agent* is a fictional creation designed to fulfil certain thematic and structural functions and capable of achieving an urbanity and irrefutability of vision which is seldom, if ever, to be enjoyed in daily life. The narrator is just as much an invention as is Marlow, the character Conrad often used to narrate his fictions in the first person.

The prose style that Conrad creates for his narrator is formal, weighty and authoritative; the tone of aloof disdain often incorporates a very sardonic kind of wit. Frequently the narrator produces something like a mock-heroic effect by suggesting an amused awareness of the gap between the punctilious, often polysyllabic and sometimes even pedantic language he adopts and the puerile nature of the characters who squirm between his forceps. (Virtually any of the narrator's more withering descriptions of Verloc would provide suitable evidence of this – see, for instance, the examples quoted on p.66.) The style of the novel gives the reader the sense of careful premeditation; every word in every sentence is precisely placed; from first to last the narrator is in control. His irony, too, manipulates our response and distances us from the characters – and from events which in some cases we would normally find unbearably gruesome or full of pathos.

Conrad has therefore created, in a novel which stresses the limitations of the perspectives of its characters, a narrator who in every possible way – and this includes the manner in which he insists on structuring the unfolding of events – asserts that *he* is the final court of appeal. He alone offers certainty, and, in his own time, the full, explicatory pattern. To be invited to share the calm, all-seeing wisdom of this narrator's own point of view, which penetrates so acutely the pretentions and obtuseness of the figures he has created, is another reason why, despite the novel's essential sombre view of existence, the reader's response is something closer to exhilaration than gloom. The heights of this ironic detachment and perception are, in the last analysis, exalting in every sense, though to achieve this lofty vision one may object that Conrad has reduced the status of most human beings in the novel to that of moral pygmies.

Perhaps the design of the novel is too reductive of human experience, but ultimately it manipulates our response into the pleasures of a comic, clear-sighted vision into a tenebrous reality and an acceptance of what may be achieved through the narrator's controlling consciousness. It is this fundamental emphasis on what may be mediated through an autonomous work of art that places Conrad in the ranks of other 'Moderns' such as Yeats or Joyce. Conrad makes it clear that it is only through the precisions and patterning of the achieved work of art that a vision of an aesthetic order may be imposed on the random, shadowy contingencies which make up our everyday experience.

7 SPECIMEN PASSAGE AND COMMENTARY

The passage chosen for discussion is taken from Chapter 12. This episode occurs shortly after Verloc's murder. Ossipon and Winnie are about to leave the shop when Winnie requests Ossipon to turn out the light in the parlour and pushes him into the room.

The curtain over the panes being drawn back a little he, by a very natural impulse, looked in, just as he made ready to turn the handle. He looked in without a thought, without intention, without curiosity of any sort. He looked in because he could not help looking in. He looked in, and discovered Mr Verloc reposing quietly on the sofa.

A yell coming from the innermost depths of his chest died out unheard and transformed into a sort of greasy, sickly taste on his lips. At the same time the mental personality of Comrade Ossipon executed a frantic leap backwards. But his body, left thus without intellectual guidance, held on to the door handle with the unthinking force of an instinct. The robust anarchist did not even totter. And he stared, his face close to the glass, his eyes protruding out of his head. He would have given anything to get away, but his returning reason informed him that it would not do to let go the door handle. What was it – madness, a nightmare, or a trap into which he had been decoyed with fiendish artfulness? Why – what for? He did not know. Without any sense of guilt in his breast, in the full peace of his conscience as far as these people were concerned, the idea that he would be murdered for mysterious reasons by the couple Verloc passed not so much across his mind as across the pit of stomach, and went out, leaving behind a trail of sickly faintness – an indisposition. Comrade Ossipon did not feel very well in a very special way for a moment – a long moment. And he stared. Mr Verloc lay very still meanwhile, simulating sleep for reasons of his own, while that savage woman of his was guarding the door – invisible and silent in the dark and deserted street. Was all this some sort of terrifying arrangement invented by the police for his especial benefit? His modesty shrank from that explanation.

But the true sense of the scene he was beholding came to Ossipon through the contemplation of the hat. It seemed an extraordinary thing, an ominous object, a sign. Black, and rim upward, it lay on the floor before the couch as if prepared to receive the contributions of pence from people who would come presently to behold Mr Verloc in the fullness of his domestic ease reposing on a sofa. From the hat the eyes of the robust anarchist wandered to the displaced table, gazed at the broken dish for a time, received a kind of optical shock from observing a white gleam under the imperfectly closed eyelids of the man on the couch. Mr Verloc did not seem so much asleep now as lying down with a bent head and looking insistently at his left breast. And when Comrade Ossipon had made out the handle of the knife he turned away from the glazed door, and retched violently.

The purpose of this section is to give some concrete demonstration of the generalisations that have already been made about the style that Conrad creates for his narrator.

Conrad's famous definition of his aim as a writer is: 'by the power of the written word to make you hear, to make you feel . . . before all, to make you *see*'. To 'see', of course, involves not merely looking with the eyes, but also *understanding* what is seen. Both elements are strongly present in this extract; from its outset, Conrad is concerned to record the unfolding of the visual impressions which force an incredulous Ossipon to a new appreciation of his situation. In terms of time measured by the clock, the experience lasts but a moment; the narrator's mode of analysis takes us through the stages of Ossipon's perception with a meticulous deliberation.

At the opening of the passage, the formula of 'looked in' is repeated four times, on one occasion twice in the same sentence, to produce a heaviness of emphasis which is also underlined by the weight of 'without a thought, without intention, without curiosity of any sort'. The reader's attention is also drawn to a portentousness in the level of diction (that is, the author's choice of words). Verloc is 'reposing' (not simply 'lying', or 'resting'); the yell comes from 'the innermost depths' of Ossipon (not from 'deep inside him'); his body 'executed' (not 'made') a leap backwards. The language suggests a formal, elevated register. Note, too, the diction and syntax (that is, the order and patterning of the words) of the second and third sentences of the second paragraph. A rough paraphrase of what is essentially said here would be something along these lines: 'Ossipon wanted to jump back, but his body would not move and he remained clutching the door handle'. More sensational versions might easily be imagined! However, at this moment of crisis, Conrad's narrator observes Ossipon's dislocated response – the split between his body and mind – with a clinical precision, and there is something intentionally circumlocutory, almost pedantic, in the expression – for instance, '. . . left him without intellectual guidance'. The constant tacking on to Ossipon's name of his revolutionary designation 'Comrade' and the use of the repeated epithet 'robust anarchist' – Ossipon is, of course, anything but 'robust' at this moment – underline a note of scorn. We pick up the cue: obviously we are meant to be amused by Ossipon's desperate attempts to come to terms with the situation. Ossipon's fixity of body while his mind goes through an extended series of thoughts (and dictates an action which he cannot perform) may indeed remind us of the 'slow-motion' of Verloc's perceptions in the moment before his murder. For Ossipon also, this will be 'a long moment'.

There is, in fact, a brief section of this extract when, in generally shorter, rather fragmented sentences, we come fairly close to being taken inside Ossipon's mind: 'What was it – madness. . . He did not know'. But almost immediately, we are watching him again 'from the outside'; the sentence structure lengthens and becomes more deliberate, and Ossipon's impressions are filtered through the narrator's attitude of sardonic remoteness from the passions described – until we reach the wry, understated comment that 'Comrade Ossipon did not feel very well in a very special way for a moment'. Then follows the amused observation that to Ossipon it appears that Verloc is 'simulating sleep for reasons of his own'.

The same note is continued later in the image which describes Verloc 'in the fullness of his domestic ease reposing on the sofa'. (Observe the precise placing of 'reposing': 'reposing in the fullness of his domestic ease on the sofa' would not give the key word the same weight.) The narrator's appreciation of irony relishes the reminder that the secret agent met death in a characteristic posture, while the image in the first part of the sentence of the hat, its rim upwards on the floor 'as if to receive the contributions of pence from people who would come presently to behold Mr Verloc' offers a typically sardonic example of the narrator's humour. By means of diction which is again knowingly inflated – 'come presently to behold Mr Verloc' – the narrator signals his own derision and invites our complicity: we are to notice the way that, with the aid of his hat, the image Verloc forms in death presents a kind of comic cartoon which neatly caricatures both the indolent and the parasitic mode of his former existence. Even in death the secret agent seems still to be scrounging his way. The image of the hat is, in fact, heavily underlined: 'It seemed an extraordinary thing, an ominous object, a sign'. It is 'extraordinary' not only, perhaps, because it jogs Ossipon into feeling that there is something odd here – Verloc was in the habit of doing most things indoors with his hat on; in its incongruous jauntiness and mockery of Verloc, the image of the hat also relates to our sense that throughout the novel objects have often seemed to take on a quirky life of their own – remember the cracked bell in the shop or the piano in the Silenus. Symbolically such objects seem to deride man's endeavours with an intrinsic absurdity and, in this case, achieve an ominous permanence which is beyond Verloc. Certainly, along with the diction and tone of the narrator, the addition of the hat to the scene that Ossipon still does not fully understand develops the note of the farcical and confirms our sense that in death Verloc is not so much an object for pity – he is more of a figure of fun.

Yet again, as Ossipon's eyes move from the hat, a most precisely constructed sentence rehearses the stages of visual awareness by which he is to be brought to enlightenment. It is the careful balancing of verbs in the sentence that is so effective: 'From the hat the eyes of the robust anarchist wandered to . . . gazed at . . . received a kind of optical shock from. . .' At this point the dead Verloc is described by the narrator as almost comically seeming to be indicating, as if to some obtuse spectator, the main point at issue: 'with a bent head and looking insistently at his left breast'.

We would normally expect the 'discovery of the murdered corpse' to provide some sensational material; it is the stuff on which the thriller writer thrives. (See how Mickey Spillane does it!) But in no sense does Conrad wish to exploit the melodramatic possibilities of the scene. He is interested in delineating the process by which Ossipon arrives at the 'true sense of the scene'; so he invites the reader to watch as if from the ringside, with his own amused detachment, an action replay of a groggy heavyweight taking in the solar plexus two enormous blows which are slowed down to make clearly visible their psychological impact – and to maximise it.

8 CRITICAL RECEPTION

Up to the time of the publication of *The Secret Agent* in September 1907, Conrad's novels had attracted a number of influential advocates of his importance as a novelist, but the books had not sold in great numbers. Until quite a late stage of his career Conrad, who always suffered intensely from the stresses and strains of writing, was financially insecure. In connection with *The Secret Agent*, he wrote to his literary agent that it was a book likely 'to produce some sensation', and he pinned considerable hope on the novel's popular success. He was to be disappointed.

There were some favourable reviews, but many reviewers felt that the novel stressed too much a squalid side of life, that there were too many 'minor and unessential characters' and that the tale was 'enormously drawn-out' or 'completely smothered by analysis'. Even praise for the novel's outstanding literary qualities was often undercut by the suggestion that, while delighting the few, its demanding structure would puzzle 'the simple reader'. In a letter to Galsworthy in January 1908, Conrad summed up his feelings: '*The Secret Agent* may be pronounced by now an honourable failure. It brought me neither love nor promise.' A few of the marks this 'failure' left are apparent in the tone Conrad adopts in his 'Author's Note' of 1920, when he refers to the admonitions and reproofs that came with the novel's first appearance.

In 1914 Richard Curle produced the first critical work of some length devoted entirely to Conrad – *Joseph Conrad: A Study*. In it he claimed that *The Secret Agent* was one of the author's major works and that 'Conrad's day is at hand and that once his sun has risen it will not set'. He was to be proved right. The years following the publication of *Chance* in 1913 saw this later novel at last gain some of the popular success Conrad had hoped *The Secret Agent* would bring him, and laudatory studies of Conrad began to appear in increasing numbers, at first particularly in the United States. H. L. Mencken, for instance, proclaimed that Conrad was pre-eminent among contemporary novelists. After the end of the First World War, in response to the growth of interest in Conrad, a series of collected editions appeared, though *The Secret Agent* did not receive its share of public or critical attention. There was still a tendency among Conrad's contemporary audience to think of him as essentially a romantic spinner of sea yarns set in exotic places, in a continuation of the Robert Louis Stevenson tradition. Such a view does a great injustice to Conrad's early work, but it may suggest why the turn his writing had taken with *Nostromo* and *The Secret Agent*, though it showed, as Walpole put it, a 'finer artist at work', was nevertheless felt by many to have 'lost something of that earlier compelling interest'.

Conrad's death on 3 August 1924 brought many acknowledgements of his genius and a number of personal accounts of the novelist – most notably Ford Madox Ford's *Joseph Conrad: A Personal Remembrance* (1924). (Ford alleges that he was instrumental in providing a good deal of the plot of *The Secret Agent*, though he is not the most reliable of sources of information.) However, the immense status Conrad currently possesses as a novelist and the judgement that *The Secret Agent*, along with *Nostromo*, represents the major part of his contribution to the English novel, still lay some time in the future. Ian Watt notes in Part I of the Macmillan Casebook on *The Secret Agent* that Conrad's profoundly pessimistic conservatism was very much out of sympathy with the prevailing radical ideology of the 1930's; the situation, however, after the Second World War made readers and critics more receptive as a result of 'disillusionment with the whole progressive political heritage, and demoralising habituation to the sordid duplicities of the Cold War'. The most centrally important work in establishing widespread critical interest in Conrad was F. R. Leavis's *The Great Tradition* (1948). Leavis, one of the most influential critics during the middle decades of the century, declared with his rigorous exclusiveness that Conrad represented, along with Jane Austen, George Eliot, Henry James and D. H. Lawrence, the only valid tradition of the English novel; he asserted that *The Secret Agent*, together with *Nostromo*, was 'one of Conrad's two supreme masterpieces, one of the two unquestionable classics of the first order that he added to the English novel'. What Leavis, of course, prized in Conrad was the intensity of moral discrimination he found there: a novelist did not gain entry to the Leavis canon without exhibiting the most profound moral seriousness. Leavis noted the subtlety of Conrad's exploration of the values of characters within *The Secret Agent's* 'cunning organisation', the 'extraordinary ironic comedy' which results, and he found in the final scene between Verloc and Winnie 'one of the most astonishing triumphs of genius in fiction'. Leavis's approach is encapsulated in the judgement that '[Conrad's] irony bears on the egocentric naïveties of moral conviction, the conventionality of conventional moral attitudes, and the obtuse assurance with which habit and self-interest assert absolute rights and wrongs'.

Since Leavis there has been an almost unanimous recognition of Conrad's status and a proliferation of approaches to *The Secret Agent*. Much criticism has concentrated on the novel's underlying political and social assumptions; some critics, such as Irving Howe, have found their radical principles affronted by what is viewed as Conrad's prejudiced and insensitive portrayal of the springs of revolutionary ideology. Other critics, like Avrom Fleishman, have explored – or imposed – a symbolic pattern which claims to produce a kind of Conradian metaphysics. Fleishman is particularly interested in the way in which the novel portrays individual consciousnesses attempting to come to terms with 'reality'. There have also been a number of psychological approaches to the novel, both Freudian and Jungian. Some of the more extreme examples of this approach – for instance Bernard C. Meyer's *Joseph Conrad: A Psychoanalytic Biography* (1967) – appear to use the novel as raw material for a slightly presumptuous case-study of Conrad's own alleged neuroses and fixations. Martin Seymour-Smith's introduction to the 1984 Penguin edition of the novel also assumes that everybody should read *The Secret Agent* in order to sharpen a diagnosis of the way in which Conrad is shedding his neurotic sicknesses and guilts. We read a lot about why Verloc is a 'transmutation' of Conrad's own situation as a writer, husband and father – and Winnie is subjected to a similar ingenious analysis as an 'objective correlative' for Conrad's wife, Jessie – but Seymour-Smith has no word to say about why the book is *made* as it is. It is odd in what purports to be a general introduction to the novel that its narrative structure and prose style should appear to be matters of no immediate interest. At this point, one can only recommend a sampling of some of the suggestions offered in the list of critical books for 'Further Reading' (see p.89). Part I of the Macmillan Casebook will provide an ideal starting-point: the editor offers a selection of contemporary reviews of *The Secret Agent* and an excellent summary of some of the more recent general trends of criticism.

REVISION QUESTIONS

1. Discuss Conrad's portrayal of the relationship between Verloc and Winnie. Account for the disastrous failure of their marriage.
2. Discuss Conrad's critique of revolutionary motivation and his characterisation of the revolutionaries in Verloc's circle of acquaintance.
3. 'Self-interest and indolence are the guiding passions of the characters in the novel.' Discuss.
4. Do you agree that we feel no sympathy for any of the characters in *The Secret Agent*?
5. 'What characters perceive as "reality" is invariably a distorted or partial version of it.' Discuss this view of the novel.
6. 'Most of the characters in *The Secret Agent* are caricatures rather than fully-rounded creations.' Discuss.
7. 'The book lacks a unifying theme, and when it is carefully examined falls apart into a succession of only superficially related scenes.' Do you agree with this assessment? Why (not)?
8. Discuss the function and importance of the 'time-switches' and the shifts in narrative perspective that we find in *The Secret Agent*.
9. 'The novel is best considered as a kind of "high-class detective story".' Should the novel be read in this way?
10. Assess the purposes and the success of Conrad's scene-setting, his evocation of atmosphere by means of the description of particular places or locales.
11. 'A thread of macabre humour and sardonic wit runs through the novel.' Discuss.
12. Discuss the uses to which Conrad puts irony in the novel.
13. 'The crucial events in the novel invariably involve a dialogue between two people.' Discuss *three* scenes of this kind and

consider the narrator's success in constructing dialogue and portraying the interaction between the characters involved.
14. Give an account of the narrator's function in *The Secret Agent*.
15. With the use of appropriate examples, define the nature and purposes of the prose style of the novel.

FURTHER READING

Conrad's writing

The essential works in the Conrad canon, besides *The Secret Agent* (1907), are probably the following:

Tales or shorter fiction: *The Nigger of the Narcissus* (1897); *Heart of Darkness* (1902); *Youth* (1902); *Typhoon* (1903); *The Secret Sharer* (1910); *The Shadow-Line* (1917).

Novels: *Lord Jim* (1900); *Nostromo* (1904); *Under Western Eyes* (1911); *Chance* (1913); *Victory* (1915).

The first two volumes of *The Collected Letters of Joseph Conrad* have been published, edited by Frederic Karl and Laurence Davies: *Volume I. Letters 1861–1897* (Cambridge University Press, 1983); *Volume II, Letters* 1898–1902 (Cambridge University Press, 1986).

Biography

Baines, Jocelyn, *Joseph Conrad: A Critical Biography* (Weidenfeld & Nicolson, 1960).
Najder, Zdzislaw, *Joseph Conrad: A Chronicle* (Cambridge University Press, 1983).
Sherry, Norman, *Conrad and His World* (Thames & Hudson, 1972).

Criticism

An essential starting-point for the student of *The Secret Agent* is the selection of essays on the novel in the Casebook Series, edited by Ian Watt (Macmillan, 1973). The following list offers a short selection of other works which contain useful information and views:

Fleishman, Avrom, *Conrad's Politics: Community and Anarchy in the Fiction of Joseph Conrad* (Johns Hopkins Press, 1967).
Guerard, Albert, *Conrad the Novelist* (Harvard University Press, 1958).
Leavis, F. R., *The Great Tradition: George Eliot; Henry James; Joseph Conrad* (Chatto & Windus, 1948).
Sherry, Norman, *Conrad's Western World* (Cambridge University Press, 1971).

Bibliography

Teets, Bruce E. & Gerber, Helmut E., *Joseph Conrad. An Annotated Bibliography of Writings about Him* (Northern Illinois University Press, 1971).